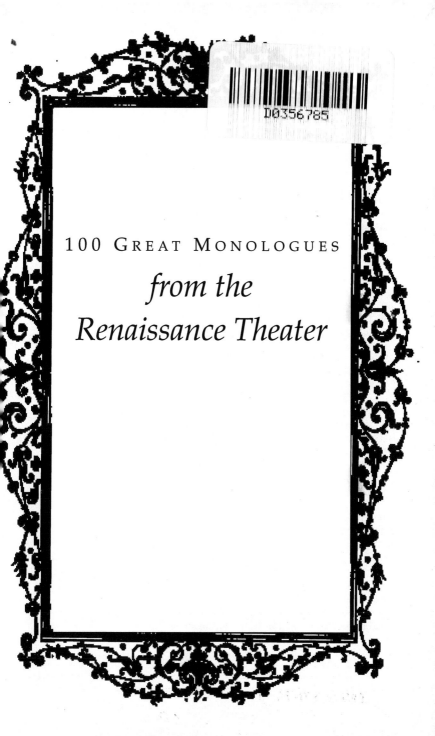

100 GREAT MONOLOGUES

from the

Renaissance Theater

MONOLOGUE AUDITION SERIES

60 Seconds to Shine Vol 1: 221 One-Minute Monologues for Men
60 Seconds to Shine Vol 2: 221 One-Minute Monologues for Women
60 Seconds to Shine Vol 3: 101 Original One-Minute Monologues by Glenn Alterman
60 Seconds to Shine Vol 4: 161 One-Minute Monologues from Literature
60 Seconds to Shine Vol 5: 101 Original One-Minute Monologues for Women Ages 18–25
60 Seconds to Shine Vol 6: 221 One-Minute Monologues from Classic Plays
The Best Men's / Women's Stage Monologues of 2006
The Best Men's / Women's Stage Monologues of 2005
The Best Men's / Women's Stage Monologues of 2004
The Best Men's / Women's Stage Monologues of 2003
The Best Men's / Women's Stage Monologues of 2002
The Best Men's / Women's Stage Monologues of 2001
The Best Men's / Women's Stage Monologues of 2000
The Best Men's / Women's Stage Monologues of 1999
The Best Men's / Women's Stage Monologues of 1998
The Best Men's / Women's Stage Monologues of 1997
The Best Men's / Women's Stage Monologues of 1996
The Best Men's / Women's Stage Monologues of 1995
The Best Men's / Women's Stage Monologues of 1994
The Best Men's / Women's Stage Monologues of 1993
The Best Men's / Women's Stage Monologues of 1992
The Best Men's / Women's Stage Monologues of 1991
The Best Men's / Women's Stage Monologues of 1990
One Hundred Men's / Women's Stage Monologues from the 1980s
2 Minutes and Under: Character Monologues for Actors Volumes I, II, and III
Monologues from Contemporary Literature: Volume I
Monologues from Classic Plays 468 BC to 1960 AD
100 Great Monologues from the Neo-Classical Theatre
100 Great Monologues from the 19th Century Romantic and Realistic Theatres
The Ultimate Audition Series Volume I: 222 Monologues, 2 Minutes & Under
The Ultimate Audition Series Volume II: 222 Monologues, 2 Minutes & Under
    from Literature
The Ultimate Audition Series Volume II: 222 Monologues, 2 Minutes & Under
    from the Movies
The Ultimate Audition Series Volume II: 222 Comedy Monologues, 2 Min & Under

YOUNG ACTOR MONOLOGUE SERIES

Great Scenes and Monologues for Children, Volumes I and II
Great Monologues for Young Actors, Volumes I and II
Short Scenes and Monologues for Middle School Actors
Multicultural Monologues for Young Actors
The Ultimate Audition Series for Middle School Actors: 111 One-Minute
Monologues Volumes I, II, and IIII
The Ultimate Audition Series for Teens: 111 One-Minute Monologues
    Volumes I, II, III, IV, V (Shakespeare), VI (by Teens)

If you would like prepublication information about upcoming Smith and Kraus books, you may receive our annual catalogue, free of charge, by sending your name and address to *Smith and Kraus Catalogue, PO Box 127, Lyme, NH 03768, call us at (888) 282-2881 or visit us at SmithandKraus.com.*

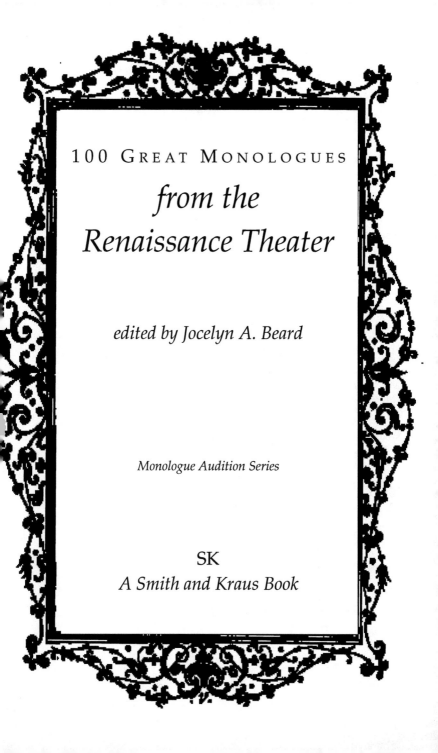

100 GREAT MONOLOGUES

from the
Renaissance Theater

edited by Jocelyn A. Beard

Monologue Audition Series

SK
A Smith and Kraus Book

*I would like to dedicate this book with love
to Marilyn Cole Green:
my mother and Renaissance gal
who taught me that "Mom" upside down is "Wow."*
—Jocelyn A. Beard

Published by Smith and Kraus Publishers, Inc.,
Hanover, NH 03755
smithandkraus.com

Copyright © 1994 by Smith and Kraus, Inc.
All rights reserved
Manufactured in the United States of America

First Edition: November 1994
9 8 7 6 5 4 3 2 1

NOTE: These monologues are intended to be used for audition and class study; permission is not required to use the material for those purposes.

Library of Congress Cataloging-in-Publication Data

100 great monologues from the Renaissance theatre / edited by Jocelyn A. Beard. --
1st ed.
          p. cm. -- (Monologue audition series)
          ISBN 1-880399-59-8 / ISBN-13 978-1-880399-59-0: $11.95
          1. Monologues. 2. Acting. 3. English drama--Early modern and Eliza
bethan. 1500-1600. I. Beard, Jocelyn. II. Title: One hundred great
monologues from the Renaissance theatre. III. Series.

PN2080.A127   1994   94-19393
822'.0450803--dc20   CIP

Contents

MEN'S RENAISSANCE MONOLOGUES

Foreword

Believe it or not, my acting cronies are constantly after me to recommend monologues for them. I am especially hard-pressed to accommodate younger performers who find themselves caught up in the middle of a grueling college audition process and figure the one person in the world who can instantly cite a "classical" monologue that would be just perfect for them - at 3:00 in the morning, no less - is me! "Whaddya mean by 'classical'?" I always grouse, knowing full well that the person calling the shots at the audition doesn't want to hear Cicero. A short definition of terms always follows, and then we arrive, as always, in the Renaissance.

That most special time in history which we have come to call the Renaissance began in Europe sometime around 1400 and lasted through the beginning of the 17th century. As a resident of Planet Earth, you're probably well acquainted with the stunning achievements in arts and letters during this time. How could you not be, for the accomplishments of the Renaissance helped to forge the cornerstone of modern civilization.

I'd like to ask you to take a moment, if you will, to contemplate the era of darkness that preceded this time of rebirth.

Europe had suffered on every level during the Dark Ages. Barbarism and disease were rampant, turning life into a commodity of little value. I mean, we're talking the Hundred Years' War, the Crusades, the Spanish Inquisition and the Great Plague. Nasty, nasty stuff. It's no great surprise that theatre during this time consisted mostly of mystery or miracle plays; Medieval dramas based on the Bible and the Apocrypha. Just take a look at Bergman's "The Seventh Seal" or "Monty Python and the Holy Grail" and you'll soon get the picture.

Wouldn't you love to have been there on the day that it all started to change?

The Renaissance arrived in Europe like a happy sigh. In England, play-wrights found a premier home in the court of Elizabeth I. Voices like Christopher Marlowe, Ben Jonson, George Peele and William Shake-speare came to be known as Elizabethan, and they sang to the world in revolutionary blank verse, proclaiming a new national identity for England, conqueror of the Spanish Armada.

By 1585, England had not one but two public theatres where plays like "Dr. Faustus," "Tamburlaine the Great" and "The Spanish Tragedy" entertained the growing non-Puritan audience. In 1588, a 24-year-old William Shakespeare leapt into the fray with the beginning of his Chronicle Plays. He then turned to farce and fantasy in plays like "The Merry Wives of Windsor" and "A Midsummer Night's Dream." Amazing.

The death of Elizabeth and the ascension to the throne of James I signaled the beginning of the Jacobean years. William Shakespeare, Ben Jonson, John Marston, John Ford and Thomas Middleton produced their greatest works during this time, leaving the world with such masterpieces as "Hamlet," "The Alchemist," "The Duchess of Malfi," "The Changeling" and "'Tis Pity She's A Whore." This was a time that was marked by religious antagonism and division. It was also the time of Copernicus and the realization that man wasn't the center of the universe after all. In theatre, comedy turned into brilliant and biting satire and tragedy became a savage study in evil and corruption. The Renaissance had taken a sharp turn towards what would eventually become the Restoration.

And so the happy sigh became a joyous shout. Voice after voice was added to the din, until the playwrights of the Renaissance had broken every restraining wall left by the dark time that had preceded it. Think of it from your own—the actor's perspective: forced for centuries to portray only saints and other Biblical personages, suddenly you can play the King of England...or the Queen! Men and women in love; men and women scheming to get what they want; treachery; incest; heroics...the actor's palate is suddenly without limit, and a new craft is born.

The Renaissance was the first era of greatness in world theatre, and the monologues in this book have all been selected with that in mind. So the next time someone tells you that you need a "classical" monologue, first make sure they don't want to hear Cicero, and then dig right in. It's all here, believe me. Don't let your experience with Renaissance Drama stop with this book. The playwrights sampled here are simply the greatest. They must be read. When the great American Bard, Cole Porter, advised us to "Brush Up Your Shakespeare," he wasn't just whistling Dixie!

Break A Leg!

Jocelyn A. Beard
Spring 1994
Patterson, NY

The Alchemist

Ben Jonson
1610

Scene: England

Female—Serio-Comic
> Dol Common: a woman of ill-repute, 30s

> When her two partners argue over who the leader of their nasty little band should be, swords are drawn and mortal threats are made. Here, Dol admonishes the two hotheads for their petty bickering.

DOL COMMON: O me!

We are ruin'd, lost! have you no more regard

To your reputations? where's your judgment? 'slight,

Have yet some care of me, of your republic—

[*FACE:* Away, this brach![1] I'll bring thee, rogue, within

The statute of sorcery, tricesimo tertio

Of Harry the eighth:[2] ay, and perhaps, thy neck

Within a noose, for laudring gold and barbing it.[3]]

DOL COMMON: (*Snatches FACE's sword.*) You'll bring your head

   within a cockscomb, will you?

And you, sir, with your menstrue[4]— (*Dashes SUBTLE's vial out of his*

   hand.) —gather it up.—

'Sdeath, you abominable pair of stinkards,

Leave off your barking, and grow one again,

Or, by the light that shines, I'll cut your throats.

I'll not be made a prey unto the marshal,

For ne'er a snarling dog-bolt[5] of you both.

Have you together cozen'd all this while,

And all the world, and shall it now be said,

You've made most courteous shift to cozen yourselves?

You will accuse him! you will bring him in (*To FACE.*)

Within the statute! Who shall take your work?

....

[1]bitch
[2]Law against witchcraft and sorcery.
[3]Washing in *aqua regia* and clipping coins.
[4]An agent by which solid substance could be dissolved.
[5]A term of contempt.

A whoreson, upstart, apocryphal captain,
Whom not a Puritan in Blackfriers will trust
So much as for a feather:[6] and you, too, (*To SUBTLE*.)
Will give the cause, forsooth! you will insult,
And claim a primacy in the divisions!
You must be chief! as if you only had
The powder to project with, and the work
Were not begun out of equality?
The venture tripartite?[7] all things in common?
Without priority? 'Sdeath! you perpetual curs,
Fall to your couples again, and cozen kindly,
And heartily, and lovingly, as you should,
And lose not the beginning of a term,[8]
Or, by this hand, I shall grow factious too,
And take my part, and quit you.

---

[6]Feathers, pins, looking glasses and other vanities were sold by Puritans in the Blackfriar section, thus the basis for frequent taunts against Puritans.

[7]Their three-member agreement: Dol, Subtle, and Face.

[8]A session of court of law, incidentally the occasion for great social activity.

Arden of Feversham

Anonymous
1592

Scene: England

#1 Female—Dramatic
   Alice: Arden's passionate young wife, 20s

   Willful Alice has been having an affair with Mosbie, a man in her husband's
   employ. When Mosbie tries to end things, Alice erupts with great fire, revealing the
   depth of her obsession.

ALICE: Is this the end of all thy solemn oaths?
Is this the fruit thy reconcilement buds?
Have I for this given thee so many favours,
Incurred my husband's hate, and, out alas!
Made shipwreck of mine honour for thy sake?
And dost thou say "henceforward know me not"?
Remember, when I lock'd thee in my closet,[9]
What were thy words and mine; did we not both
Decree to murder Arden in the night?
The heavens can witness, and the world can tell,
Before I saw that falsehood look of thine,
'Fore I was tangled with thy 'ticing[10] speech,
Arden to me was dearer than my soul,—
And shall be still: base peasant, get thee gone,
And boast not of thy conquest over me,
Gotten by witchcraft and mere[11] sorcery!
For what hast thou to countenance my love,
Being descended of a noble house,
And matched already with a gentleman
Whose servant thou may'st be!—and so farewell.

---

[9]private room
[10]enticing
[11]absolute

> Following a botched attempt to murder her husband, Alice here does her best to convince him of her innocence.

ALICE: Ah, Arden, what folly blinded thee?
Ah, jealous harebrained man, what has thou done!
When we, to welcome thee with intended sport,
Came lovingly to meet thee on thy way,
Thou drew'st thy sword, enraged with jealousy,
And hurt thy friend whose thoughts were free from harm;
All for a worthless kiss and joining arms,
Both done but merrily to try thy patience.
And me unhappy that devised the jest,
Which though begun in sport, yet ends in blood!
[*FRANKLIN:* Marry, God defend me from such a jest!]
ALICE: Could'st thou not see us friendly smile on thee,
When we joined arms, and when I kissed his cheek?
Hast thou not lately found me over-kind?
Did'st thou not hear me cry "they murder thee"?
Called I not help to set my husband free?
No, ears and all were witched; ah me accursed
To link in liking with a frantic man!
Henceforth I'll be thy slave, no more thy wife,
For with that name I never shall content thee.
If I be merry, thou straightways think me light;
If sad, thou sayest the sullens[12] trouble me;
If well attired, thou thinks I will be gadding;
If homely, I seem sluttish[13] in thine eye:
Thus am I still, and shall be while[14] I die.
Poor wench abused by thy misgovernment!

---

[12]gloomy ill-humor
[13]untidy
[14]until

Cambyses, King of Persia

Thomas Preston
1569–70

Scene: Persia

Female—Dramatic
   Mother: a woman discovering the cruel death of her young son, 20–30

   When the king's counsel, Praxaspes, criticizes the king's drinking, the enraged ruler demands that Praxaspes' young son stand at a distance so that he may shoot at him with a bow and arrow. He strikes the boy in the heart claiming that such a feat could not have been accomplished by a drunken man. Here, the boy's mother discovers his body.

MOTHER: Alas, alas, I do hear tell the King hath killed my son.
If it be so, woe worth the deed that ever it was done.
It is even so. My lord I see, how by him he doth weep.
What meant I that from hands of him this child I did not keep?
Alas, husband and lord, what did you mean to fetch this child away?
[*PRAXASPES:* O lady wife, I little thought for to have seen this day.]
MOTHER: O blissful babe! O joy of womb! Heart's comfort and
   delight!
For counsel given unto the king is this thy just requite?
O heavy day and doleful time, these mourning tunes to make!
With blubb'red eyes into mine arms from earth I will thee take
And wrap thee in mine apron white. But, O my heavy heart!
The spiteful pangs that it sustains would make it in two to part,
The death of this my son to see. Oh heavy mother now,
That from thy sweet and sug'rèd joy to sorrow so shouldst bow!
What grief in womb did I retain before I did thee see!
Yet at last, when smart was gone, what joy wert thou to me!
How tender was I of thy food, for to preserve thy state!
How stillèd I thy tender heart at times early and late!
With velvet paps I gave thee suck with issue from my breast,
And dancèd thee upon my knee to bring thee unto rest.
Is this the joy of thee I reap? O king of tiger's brood!
O tiger's whelp, hadst thou the heart to see this child's heart-blood?
Nature enforceth me, alas, in this wise to deplore,
To wring my hands. Oh wellaway, that I should see this hour!

Thy mother yet will kiss thy lips, silk-soft and pleasant white,
With wringing hands lamenting for to see thee in this plight.
My lording dear, let us go home our mourning to augment.

David and Bethsabe

George Peele
1599

Scene: Israel

Female—Dramatic
   Bethsabe: wife of Urias, desired by King David, 20–30

   David's illicit passion for Bethsabe leads him to engineer her husband's death in
   battle. Here, tormented by feelings of guilt and grief, the widowed Bethsabe laments
   her loss.

BETHSABE: Mourn, Bethsabe, bewail thy foolishness,
Thy sin, thy shame, the sorrow of thy soul.
Sin, shame, and sorrow swarm about thy soul;
And in the gates and entrance of my[15] heart
Sadness, with wreathèd arms, hangs her complaint.
No comfort from the ten-stringed instrument,
The tinkling[16] cymbal, or the ivory lute;
Nor doth the sound of David's kingly harp
Make glad the broken heart of Bethsabe.
Jerusalem is filled with thy complaint,
And in the streets of Sion sits thy grief.
The babe is sick, sick to the death, I fear,
The fruit that sprung from thee to David's house;
Nor may the pot of honey and of oil
Glad David or his handmaid's countenance.
Urias—woe is me to think hereon!
For who is it among the sons of men
That saith not to my soul, "The King hath sinned;
David hath done amiss, and Bethsabe
Laid snares of death unto Urias' life"?
My sweet Urias, fallen into the pit
Art thou, and gone even to the gates of hell
For Bethsabe, that wouldst not shroud her shame.

---

[15]my Q
[16]twinkling Q

Oh, what is it to serve the lust of kings!
How lion-like th[e]y rage when we resist!
But, Bethsabe, in humbleness attend
The grace that God will to his handmaid send.

The Deceived

Gl'Intronati Di Siena
1538

Scene: Modena

#1 Female—Serio-Comic
> Lelia: a young girl masquerading as a boy, 14–16

> Lelia has run away from the convent in order to help the man she loves to woo another woman. Here, she steals through the city streets fearing that she may be accosted by a group of young men.

LELIA: I can't think where I found the nerve to come out alone like this at this time of day, knowing what I do about the bad habits of the wicked young men of Modena! It would serve me right if one of those reckless young idiots grabbed hold of me and dragged me into a house somewhere to find out whether I'm really a boy or a girl! That would teach me to go out on my own in the early hours like this! But the cause of all this turmoil is my love for that ungrateful brute Flamminio. Talk about back luck! I'm in love with a man who hates me and never has a good word for me; I serve a man who doesn't even know who I am! And to make things worse, I'm helping him to court another girl, without a hope—and this is what no one will ever believe—without a hope of any satisfaction beyond what I can get out of feasting my eyes on him! Well, it's worked all right so far; but what can I do now? What plan am I to follow? My father's come home and Flamminio's come to live in town—and I can't go on like this in Modena without being recognized. And if I am, I shall be ruined for ever, and become a byword in the whole city. And that's why I've come out so early, to consult my nurse. I was looking out of the window, and saw her coming this way, and I want to ask her to help me choose the best course of action. But first of all let's see if she knows me in these clothes.

#2 Female—Serio-Comic
> Pasquella: a maid servant, 50–60

> When Pasquella is sent on yet another errand by her love-sick mistress, she takes a moment to rue the ravages of young love.

PASQUELLA: (*Aside.*) I don't believe any job in the world can be more difficult or more unpleasant for someone like me than serving a young lady who's in love—especially one who's got no mother, sisters or anyone else to keep her in check—and that's my mistress. These last few days she's got such a passion, such an itch of love on her that she can't stay still either by day or by night. All the time she's scratching herself where it itches, she's stroking her things, she's running to the loggia, she's dashing to the window, and upstairs and downstairs—it's as if she had quicksilver under her feet. Heaven help us! I've been young and in love myself, and managed to do a little something about it, too; but I used to get some rest from time to time, even then. At least she might have taken a fancy to a proper man—someone who'd reached maturity, as they say, and would have known what to do with himself and been able to get all this nonsense out of her system. But she's got involved with a young sprig who looks as if he'd hardly know how to do up his own clothes without help, if they came undone. And all day long she sends me out to look for this fine lover of hers—as if I hadn't plenty of work to do in the house. Can Flamminio really believe that all these messages to and fro are for his benefit? But I believe that's the boy coming in this direction now. That's lucky! Fabio! God send you a good day! I was just coming to look for you, my pet.

#3 Female—Serio-Comic
    Pasquella

> Willful Lelia has been masquerading as a boy in order to win the love of Flamminio. When her long-lost brother, Fabrizio returns to Modena, he is mistaken for Lelia by their father. Thinking that he has finally captured the wayward Lelia, their father locks up Fabrizio with the beautiful young Isabella. Here, Pasquella describes the shocking scene that greeted her when she unlocked Isabella's door to see how the two "girls" were doing.

PASQUELLA: (*Soliloquizing.*) Oh dear! Oh dear! I've had such a fright, I had to run out into the street! And really, dear ladies (*Addressing female members of the audience.*) —if I didn't tell you what happened, you'd never guess. But I'll tell you about it, sweet ladies, and not those horrible men, who'd only laugh. Those two old idiots would have it that the young fellow was really a girl, and they locked him up in the downstairs bedroom with my young mistress Isabella, and gave me the key. I thought I'd go in and see what they were doing; and I found them hugging and kissing like mad. That made me want to make sure whether he really was a boy or a girl. Well, my mistress had got him stretched out on the bed, and she called out and asked me to help her while she held his hands; and then he stopped resisting. So I undid him in front; and suddenly something flew up and hit me across the knuckles, and I couldn't tell whether it was a pestle, or a carrot, or one of those other things. But whatever else it might have been, it certainly wasn't undernourished! When I saw what it looked like, I could see this was a case of devil take the hindmost, and away I ran. I'm sure I wouldn't dare to go back into that room myself; but if any of you ladies doesn't believe me and wants to see for yourself, I'll lend her the key.— But here's Giglio. I must see if I can manage things so that I get the rosary and make a fool of him. These Spaniards think they're so clever that they can't believe anyone in the world's a match for them.

The Devil's Law-Case

John Webster

1623

Scene: Naples

Female—Dramatic
  Leonora: a grieving woman, 40s

Here, passionate Leonora is driven mad with grief at the news that her son has murdered Contarino, a nobleman with whom she was very much in love.

LEONORA: Stay, will you mourn for Contarino?
[*ROMELIO:* O, by all means; 'tis fit—my sister is his heir.]
LEONORA: I will make you chief mourner, believe it.
Never was woe like mine, O, that my care
And absolute study to preserve his life
Should be his absolute ruin! Is he gone then?
There is no plague i'th' world can be compared
To impossible desire, for they are plagued[17]
In the desire itself. Never, O never
Shall I behold him living, in whose life
I lived far sweetlier than in mine own.
A precise curiosity has undone me: why did I not[18]
Make my love known directly? 'T had not been
Beyond example for a matron
To affect i'th' honorable way of marriage[19]
So youthful a person. O, I shall run mad!
For as we love our youngest children best,
So the last fruit of our affection,
Wherever we bestow it, is most strong,
Most violent, most unresistable,
Since 'tis indeed our latest harvest-home,
Last merriment 'fore winter; and we widows,
As men report of our best picture-makers,
We love the piece we are in hand with better

---

[17]Those who desire.
[18]Overtly subtle behavior.
[19]Seek after.

Than all the excellent work we have done before.
And has my son depriv'd me of all this. Ha, my son!
I'll be a fury to him; like an Amazon lady,
I'd cut off this right pap, that gave him suck,
To shoot him dead.[20] I'll no more tender him,[21]
Than had a wolf stol'n to my teat i'th' night
And robbed me of my milk; nay, such a creature
I should love better far.— Ha, ha, what say you?
I do talk to somewhat, methinks; it may be
My evil genius. Do not the bells ring?
I have a strange noise in my head: O, fly in pieces![22]
Come, age, and wither me into the malice
Of those that have been happy; let me have
One property more than the devil of hell,
Let me envy the pleasure of youth heartily;
Let me in this life fear no kind of ill,
That have no good to hope for. Let me die
In the distraction of that worthy princess[23]
Who loathed food, and sleep, and ceremony,
For thought of losing that brave gentleman
She would fain have saved, had not a false conveyance[24]
Express'd him stubborn-hearted.[25]
Let me sink where neither man
Nor memory may ever find me.

---

[20]These warrior women reputedly had the right breast removed to facilitate drawing a bowstring.

[21]Feel tenderly toward.

[22]Like an old, overcharged cannon (Lucas).

[23]An early reference to the romanticized story of Queen Elizabeth's mourning for Essex's death. The Countess of Nottingham confessed she had not passed on a ring Essex had sent the Queen in suit for pardon, and had made him seem intransigent (Lucas).

[24]Transmittal, with an overtone of furtive action.

[25]Made him appear.

A Fair Quarrel

Thomas Middleton and William Rowley
1617

Female—Dramatic
>   Lady Ager: a woman trying to protect her son, 40–50

>   When her son is accused of being illegitimate, he challenges his accuser to a duel.
>   Here, the distraught Lady Ager fears for the loss of her son.

LADY AGER: Oh, he's lost, he's gone!
For all my pains, he's gone; two meeting torrents
Are not so merciless as their two rages.
He never comes again.— (*Aside.*) Wretched affection!
Have I belied my faith, injur'd my goodness,
Slander'd my honor for his preservation,
Having but only him, and yet no happier?
'Tis then a judgment plain; truth's angry with me,
In that I would abuse her sacred whiteness
For any worldly temporal respect.
Forgive me, then, thou glorious woman's virtue,
Admir'd where'er thy habitation is,
Especially in us weak ones! Oh, forgive me,
For 'tis thy vengeance this. To belie truth,
Which is so hardly ours, with such pain purchas'd,
Fastings and prayers, continence and care!
Misery must needs ensue. Let him not die
In that unchaste belief of his false birth
And my disgrace! Whatever angel guides him,
May this request be with my tears obtain'd:
Let his soul know my honor is unstain'd.—
Run, seek, away! If there be any hope,
Let me not lose him yet! When I think on him,
His dearness, and his worth, it earns[26] me more;
They that know riches tremble to be poor.

....

[26]grieves

My passion is not every woman's sorrow;
She must be truly honest feels my grief,
And only known to one.[27] If such there be,
They know the sorrow that oppresseth me.

---

[27]One man (Sampson). The sense of the phrase is "faithful to one man."

The Faithful Shepherd

Giambattista Guarini

1590

Scene: Arcadia

#1 Female—Dramatic
Corisca: a wanton nymph, 20s

> Corisca has fallen in love with Mirtillo, who is himself in love with the beautiful
> Amarillis. When her passion remains unrequited, the fiery nymph vows to win his
> heart and make all suffer.

CORISCA: Who ever saw, what heart did ever prove
So strange, fond, impotent a passion? Love,
And cold disdain (a miracle to me
Two contraries should in one subject be
Both in extremes!) I know not how, each other
Destroy and generate, inflame and smother.
When I behold Mirtillo's every grace,
From his neat foot to his bewitching face,
His unaffected carriage, sweet aspect,
Words, actions, looks and manners, they eject
Such flames of love, that every passion
Besides seems to be conquered by this one.
But when I think how dotingly he prizes
Another woman, and for her despises
My almost peerless face (although I say't)
On which a thousand eyes for alms do wait,
Then do I scorn, abhor, and loathe him more
Than ever I did value him before,
And scarce can think it possible that he
Had ever any interest for me.
Oh, if my sweet Mirtillo were mine own,
So that I had him to myself alone
(These are my thoughts sometimes) no mortal wight
More bliss could boast of than Corisca might!
And then I feel such kindly flames, so sweet

A vapour rise, that I could almost meet
His love halfway; yea, follow him, adore
His very steps, and aid from him implore:
Nay, I do love him so, I could expire
His sacrifice in such a pleasing fire.
Then I'm myself again; and "What!" say I,
"A proud disdainful boy! One that doth fly
From me and love another! that can look
Upon this face of mine, and not be struck,
But guard himself so well as not to die
For love! Shall I, that should behold him lie
Trembling and weeping at these feet of mine
(As many better men have done) incline
Trembling and weeping at *his* feet? Oh, no!"
And with this thought into such rage I grow
Against myself, and him, that sounding straight
Unto my eyes and fancy a retreat,
Mirtillo's name worser than death I seem
To hate, and mine own self for loving him;
Whom I would see the miserablest swain,
The most despised thing that doth remain
Upon the earth; and if I had my will,
With my own hands I could the villain kill.
Thus like two seas encountering, hate and love,
Desire and scorn in me dire battle move:
And I (the flame of thousand hearts, the rack
Of thousand souls) languish, and burn, and lack
That pity I denied to others. I
Who have in cities oft been courted by
Gallants and wits, to whom great lords have bent,
And yet withstood volleys of compliment,
Squadrons of lovers, jeered their idle fires,
And with false hopes deluded their desires;
And now enforced to a rustic swain to yield!
In single fight to a fellow that's unskilled!
O thou most wretched of all womankind

Corisca! Where couldst thou diversion find
Hadst thou no other lover? How assuage,
Or by what means deceive thy amorous rage?
Learn women all from me this housewifery:
Make you conserve of lovers to keep by.
Had I no sweetheart but this sullen boy,
Were I not well provided of a joy?
To extreme want how likely to be hurled
Is that ill housewife, who in all the world
But one love only, but one servant hath?
Corisca will be no such fool. What's faith?
What's constancy? Tales which the jealous feign
To awe fond girls—names as absurd as vain.
Faith in a woman (if at least there be
Faith in a woman unrevealed to me)
Is not a virtue, nor a heavenly grace,
But the sad penance of a ruined face,
That's pleased with one, 'cause it can please no more;
A handsome woman sought unto by store
Of gallant youths, if pleased with one alone
No woman is, or is a foolish one.
What's beauty, tell me, if not viewed? or viewed,
If not pursued? or if pursued, pursued
By one alone? Where lovers frequent are,
It is a sign the party loved is rare,
Glorious and bright. A woman's honour is
To have many servants: courtly dames know this,
Who live in towns, and those most practice it
Who have most wealth, most beauty, and most wit.
'Tis clownishness, they say, to reject any,
And folly too, since that's performed by many,
One cannot do: one officer to wait,
A second to present,[28] a third to prate,
A fourth for somewhat else; so it doth fall

[28]Give presents.

Out oft, that favours being general
No favours seem: or jealousy thus thrown
To whet them, all are easier kept than one.
This merry life is by great ladies led
In towns, and 'twas my fortune to be bred
With one of them, by whose example first,
Next by her rules, I in love's art was nurst
Up from my childhood; she would often say:
"Corisca, thou must use another day
"Thy lovers like thy garments—put on one,
"Have many, often shift, and wear out none.
"For daily conversation breeds distaste,
"Distaste contempt, and loathing at the last.
"Then get the start, let not the servant say
"He's turned his mistress, not she him, away."
And I have kept her rules: I've choice, and strive
To please them all: to this my hand I give,
And wink on him; the handsom'st I admit
Into my bosom; but not one shall get
Into my heart: and yet (I know not how)
Ay me! Mirtillo's crept too near it now.
He made me sigh—not sigh as heretofore,
To give false fire, but true flames to deplore,
Robbing my limbs of rest, my eyes of sleep,
Even I can watch till the grey morning peep
(The discontented lover's truce); even I
(Strange change!) to melancholy walks can fly;
And through the gloomy horrors of this grove
Trace the sweet footsteps of my hated love.
What wilt thou do, Corisca? Sue? My hate
Permits not this, nor stands it with my state.
Wilt thou then fly him? That would show more brains,
But love says no to that. What then remains?
First I will try allurements, and discover
The love to him, but will conceal the lover.
I'll use deceits, if that avail me not;

And if those fail me too, my brain shall plot
A brave revenge; Mirtillo shall partake
Hate, if he spurn at love, and I will make
His Amarillis rue that she was e'er
A rival unto me, and him so dear.
Last I will teach you both what 'tis to move
A woman to abhor where she did love.

#2 Female—Dramatic
> Amarillis: a young woman in love, 16–20

> Here, Amarillis greets the day with great joy in her heart while reflecting upon
> the inner wealth that poverty may provide for the spirit.

AMARILLIS: Dear happy groves, and you ye solitary
And silent woodlands where true peace doth tarry,
With how much joy do I review you! And
Had my stars pleased to give me the command
Over my self, that I might choose my lot,
And my own way of life, then would I not
For the Elysian groves, about which range
The happy shades, your happy shades exchange.
For what we foolish mortals "goods" do call,
If rightly understood, are evils all.
He that hath most of them, in truth hath least,
Nor is so much possessor, as possessed;
Not riches, no, but of our freedom snares.
What boots it in the springtime of one's years
To have the attributes of fair and good,
In mortal veins to lock celestial blood,
Graces of body and of mind; here fair
And laughing fields of corn, rich meadows there,
In fruitful pasture-grounds more fruitful flocks,
If with all these the heart contentment lacks?
Happy that shepherdess whom some coarse stuff
Obscurely clothes, yet clean and just enough!
Rich only in herself, and bravely dressed
With nature's ornaments, which are the best;

Who in sweet poverty no want doth know,
Nor the distractions which from riches grow;
Yet whatsoever may suffice the mind
In that estate abundantly doth find;
Poor, but content! with nature's gifts retrieves
The gifts of nature, milk with milk revives,
And with the sweet which from the bee she gets
Seasons the honey of her native sweets.
One fountain is her looking-glass, her drink,
Her bath; and if she's pleased, what others think
It matters not; she heeds not blazing stars
That threaten mighty ones: wars or no wars,
It is all one to her; her battlement
And shield is that she's poor: *Poor, but content!*
One only care—'tis a sweet care—doth keep
Her heart awake: she feeds her master's sheep
With pearléd grass, and with her lovely eyes
Some honest swain, that for her beauty dies—
Not such as men or gods choose to her hand,
But such as love did to her choice commend,
And in some favoured shady myrtle grove
Desires and is desired, nor feels of love
One spark which unto him she doth not show,
Nor shows one spark with which he doth not glow.
Poor, but content! True life, which till the breath
Forsakes the body, knowst not what is death.
Would Heaven had made me such a one! But see,
Corisca! Sweet Corisca!

#3 Female—Dramatic
    Amarillis

> Although Amarillis is promised in marriage to Silvio, her heart belongs to Mirtillo.
> During an innocent game of blind man's bluff, Mirtillo tricks Amarillis into kissing
> him. When she realizes that she has been deceived, she chastises him as best she can.

AMARILLIS: To answer thee if I had promiséd,
As well as hear thee, this were justly said.
Thou callst me cruel, hoping that, to shun

That vice, into the contrary I'll run.
But know, my ears are not so tickléd
With that (by me so little merited
And less desiréd) praise thou givst to me
Of beauty, as to hear myself by thee
Styled "cruel"—which to be to any other,
I grant were vice; 'tis virtue to a lover.
And what thou harshness callst and cruelty
Is in a woman perfect honesty.
But say that e'en to a love 'twere a sin—
Yet tell me, when hath Amarillis bin
Cruel to thee? Was't then when justice bad
To use no pity, yet on thee I had
So much, that I from death delivered thee?
I mean, when 'mongst a noble company
Of modest virgins mingled, thou didst cover
With a maid's habit a libidinous lover;
And, our chaste sports polluting, didst intrude
'Mongst kisses feigned and innocent thy lewd
And wanton kisses—such an act as yet
I blush as oft as I but think on it.
But at that time I knew thee not, heaven knows,
And when I did my indignation rose.
Thy wantonness I from my mind did keep,
And suffered not the amorous plague to creep
To my chaste heart; on my lips' outer skin
The poison stuck, but none of it got in.
A mouth that's kissed perforce,
If it spit out the kiss, is ne'er the worse.
But what wouldst thou by that bold theft have got
If I had to those nymphs discovered what
Thou wert? The Thracian women never tore
And murdered Orpheus so on Hebrus' shore,
As they had thee, unless her clemency
Whom thou callst cruel now had rescued thee.
But she is not so cruel as she ought

To be: for if when she is cruel thought
Thy boldness is so great, what would it be
If she were judgéd pitiful by thee?
That honest pity which I could, I gave;
Other it is in vain for thee to crave,
Or hope: for amorous pity she can ill
Bestow, who gave it all to one that will
Give her none back. If thou my lover be,
Love my good name, my life, my honesty.
Thou seekst impossibles; I am a ward
To Heaven, Earth watches me, and my reward,
If I transgress, is death; but most of all,
Virtue defends me with a brazen wall.
For she that is protected by her honour,
Scorns there should be a safer guard upon her.
Look to thy safety, then, and do not give
Battle to me, Mirtillo; fly, and live
If thou be wise. For out of sense of smart
To abandon life, argues but a faint heart.
And 'tis the part of virtue to abstain
From what we love, if it will prove our bane.

#4 Female—Dramatic
    Amarillis

> After she has sent Mirtillo away, Amarillis laments their impossible love for one
> another.

AMARILLIS: Mirtillo, O Mirtillo, couldst thou see
That heart which thou condemn'st of cruelty
—Soul of my soul!—thou unto it wouldst show
That pity which thou begst from it, I know.
Oh ill-starred lovers! what avails it me
To have thy love! T'have mine, what boots it thee?
Whom love hath joined why dost thou separate,
Malicious fate? And two divorced by fate
Why joinst thou, perverse love? How blest are you
Wild beasts that are in loving tied unto

No laws but those of love! whilst human laws
Inhumanly condemn us for that cause.
Oh why, if this be such a natural
And powerful passion, was it capital?
Nature too frail, that dost with law contend!
Law too severe, that nature dost offend!
But what? they love but little who death fear!
Ah, my Mirtillo, would to heaven that were
The only penalty! Virtue, which art
The binding'st law to an ingenuous heart,
This inclination which in me I feel,
Lanced with the sharp point of thy holy steel,
To thee I sacrifice: and pardon, dear
Mirtillo, her that's only cruel where
She must not pity. Pardon thy fierce foe
In looks and words—but in her heart not so.
Or if addicted to revenge thou be,
What greater vengeance canst thou take on me
Than thine own grief? For if thou be my heart,
As in despite of heaven and earth thou art,
Thy sign my vital spirits are, the flood
Of tears which follows is my vital blood,
And all these pangs, and all these groans of thine
Are not thy pangs, are not thy groans, but mine.

#5 Female—Dramatic
    Corisca

> When Amarillis confesses her forbidden love for Mirtillo to the scheming Corisca,
> the nymph does her best to incite the unhappy young woman to risk death by
> defying her contracted engagement to Silvio.

CORISCA: Thou art too nice: if women all were such,
And on these scruples should insist so much,
Good days adieu! I hold them simple souls
Will live obnoxious to such poor controls.
Laws are not for the wise: if to be kind
Should merit death, Jove help the cruel mind![29]

But if fools fall into those snares, 'tis fit
They be forbid to steal, who have not wit
To hide their theft. For honesty is but
An art, an honest gloss on vice to put.
Think others as they list; thus I conceive.
[*AMARILLIS:* These rotten grounds, Corisca, will deceive.
What I can't hold 'tis wisdom soon to quit.]
CORISCA: And who forbids thee, fool? Our life doth flit
Too fast away to lose one jot of it;
And men so squeamish and so curious grown,
That two of our new lovers make not one
O' th' old. We are no longer for their tooth
—Believe't—that while we're new. Bate us our youth,
Bate us our beauty, and, like hollow trees
Which had been stuffed with honey by the bees,
If that by lickerish hands away be ta'en,
Dry and despiséd trunks we shall remain.
Therefore let them have leave to babble what
They please, as those who know nor reckon not
What the poor woman Amarillis bears.
Our case alas is differing much from theirs.
Men in perfection as in age increase,
Wisdom supplies the lack of handsomeness:
But when our youth and beauty, which alone
Conquer the strength and wit of men, are gone,
All's gone with us; nor canst thou possibly
Say a worse thing, or to be pardoned thee
More hardly, than "old woman." Then before
Thou split on that unevitable shore,
Know thine own worth, and do not be so mad,
As when thou mayst live merry, to live sad.
What would the lion's strength boot him, or wit
Avail a man, unless he uséd it?
Our beauty is to us that which to men

. . . .

[29]In this couplet Fanshawe has introduced a completely new idea of his own. The Italian simply says that if the law were enforced with rigor, there would be no women left alive in Arcadia at all.

Wit is, or strength unto the lion. Then
Let us use it while we may,
Snatch those joys that haste away.
Earth her winter-coat may cast,
And renew her beauty past;
But, our winter come, in vain
We solicit spring again;
And when our furrows snow shall cover,
Love may return, but never lover.

Gallathea

John Lyly
1583–85

Scene: mythological Tudor England

#1 Female—Serio-Comic
Telusa: a nymph of the goddess, Diana, 18–20

When the virgin nymph of chaste Diana feels the first stirrings of romantic passion,
she agonizes over her maidenly state.

TELUSA: How now? What new conceits,[30] what strange contraries,
breed in thy mind? Is thy Diana become a Venus, thy chaste thoughts
turned to wanton looks, thy conquering modesty to a captive imagina-
tion? Beginnest thou with pyralis[31] to die in the air and live in the fire,
to leave the sweet delight of hunting and to follow the hot desire of
love? O Telusa, these words are unfit for thy sex, being a virgin, but apt
for thy affections, being a lover. And can there in years so young, in
education so precise, in vows so holy, and in a heart so chaste enter
either a strong desire or a wish or a wavering thought of love? Can
Cupid's brands[32] quench Vesta's[33] flames, and his feeble shafts headed
with feathers pierce deeper than Diana's arrows headed with steel?
Break thy bow, Telusa, that seekest to break thy vow, and let those
hands that aimed to hit the wild hart scratch out those eyes that have
wounded thy tame heart. O vain and only[34] naked name of chastity,
that is made[35] eternal and perisheth by time; holy, and is infected by
fancy; divine, and is made mortal by folly! Virgins' hearts, I perceive,
are not unlike cotton trees, whose fruit is so hard in the bud that it
soundeth like steel, and, being ripe, poureth forth nothing but wool,
and their thoughts like the leaves of lunary,[36] which, the further they
grow from the sun, the sooner they are scorched with his beams. O
Melebeus, because thou art fair must I be fickle, and false my vow

[30]fancy
[31]A fabulous fly supposed to live in or be generated by fire and to die out of the flame.
[32]torches
[33]Vesta was a Roman hearth-goddess, in whose temple virgins tended a sacred fire.
[34]Of itself alone.
[35]Made out to be.
[36]The plant moonwort.

because I see thy virtue? Fond girl that I am, to think of love; nay, vain profession that I follow, to disdain love! But here cometh Eurota. I must now put on a red mask and blush, lest she perceive my pale face and laugh.

#2 Female—Dramatic
Diana: goddess of the hunt, 20s

When Diana discovers that her virgin nymphs have all allowed themselves to fall in love, she lectures them on the importance of remaining chaste.

DIANA: Now, ladies, doth not that make your cheeks blush that makes mine ears glow, or can you remember that without sobs which Diana cannot think on without sighs? What greater dishonor could happen to Diana, or to her nymphs shame, than that there can be any time so idle that should make their heads so addle? Your chaste hearts, my nymphs, should resemble the onyx, which is hottest when it is whitest, and your thoughts, the more they are assaulted with desires, the less they should be affected. You should think love like Homer's moly,[37] a white leaf and a black root, a fair show and a bitter taste. Of all trees the cedar is greatest and hath the smallest seeds; of all affections love hath the greatest name and the least virtue. Shall it be said, and shall Venus say it, nay, shall it be seen, and shall wantons see it, that Diana, the goddess of chastity, whose thoughts are always answerable to her vows, whose eyes never glanced on desire, and whose heart abateth[38] the point of Cupid's arrows, shall have her virgins to become unchaste in desires, immoderate in affection, untemperate in love, in foolish love, in base love? Eagles cast their evil feathers in the sun, but you cast your best desires upon a shadow. The birds Ibes[39] lose their sweetness when they lose their sights, and virgins all their virtues with their unchaste thoughts. Unchaste Diana calleth that that hath either any show or suspicion of lightness. O my dear nymphs, if you knew how loving thoughts stain lovely faces, you would be as careful to have the one as unspotted as the other beautiful.

....

[37]Herb given by Hermes to Odysseus to prevent the enchantress Circe's magic from turning him into an animal as it did his men.
[38]turns aside, blunts
[39]Long-legged, slender-billed birds venerated in ancient Egypt; the singular form is "ibis."
[40]Women who prostituted themselves in service of the love-goddess.

Cast before your eyes the loves of Venus' trulls,[40] their fortunes, their fancies, their ends. What are they else but Silenus' pictures[41] without, lambs and doves within, apes and owls, who like Ixion embrace clouds for Juno,[42] the shadows of virtue instead of the substance? The eagle's feathers consume the feathers of all others, and love's desire corrupteth all other virtues. I blush, ladies, that you, having been heretofore patient of labors, should now become prentices to idleness, and use the pen for sonnets, not the needle for samplers. And how is your love placed? Upon pelting[43] boys, perhaps base of birth, without doubt weak of discretion. Ay, but they are fair. O ladies, do your eyes begin to love colors,[44] whose hearts was wont to loath them? Is Diana's chase[45] become Venus' court, and are your holy vows turned to hollow thoughts?

#3 Female—Dramatic
> Hebe: a virgin about to be sacrificed to a monster, 16–20

> Hebe has been selected to be sacrificed to the monster, Agar, to appease Neptune. As she is led to her doom, she bids farewell to life.

HEBE: Miserable and accursed Hebe, that, being neither fair nor fortunate, thou shouldst be thought most happy and beautiful. Curse thy birth, thy life, thy death, being born to live in danger, and, having lived, to die by deceit. Art thou the sacrifice to appease Neptune and satisfy the custom,[46] the bloody custom, ordained for the safety of thy country? Ay, Hebe, poor Hebe, men will have it so, whose forces command our weak natures. Nay, the gods will have it so, whose powers dally with our purposes. The Egyptians never cut their dates from the tree because they are so fresh and green. It is thought wickedness to pull roses from the stalks in the garden of Palestine, for that they have so lively a red; and whoso cutteth the incense tree in Arabia, before it fall, committeth sacrilege.

---

[41]In classical Athens, busts of the ugly satyr contained images of gods.
[42]When Ixion attempted to seduce Zeus's wife Hera, Zeus substituted a cloud-image of her, on which the seducer begat the Centaurs, or their father, and was punished by being chained to a revolving wheel.
[43]paltry
[44]Complexions, appearances.
[45]Hunting-ground.
[46]Tradition, tribute.

Shall it only be lawful amongst us in the prime of youth and pride of beauty to destroy both youth and beauty, and what was honored in fruits and flowers as a virtue to violate in a virgin as a vice? But alas, destiny alloweth no dispute. Die, Hebe, Hebe, die, woeful Hebe and only accursed Hebe. Farewell the sweet delights of life, and welcome now the bitter pangs of death. Farewell, you chaste virgins, whose thoughts are divine, whose faces fair, whose fortunes are agreeable to your affections, Enjoy and long enjoy the pleasure of your curled locks, the amiableness of your wished looks, the sweetness of your tuned voices, the content of your inward thoughts, the pomp of your outward shows. Only Hebe biddeth farewell to all the joys that she conceived and you hope for, that she possessed and you shall. Farewell the pomp of prince's courts whose roofs are embossed with gold and whose pavements are decked with fair ladies, where the days are spent in sweet delights, the nights in pleasant dreams, where chastity honoreth affections and commandeth, yieldeth to desire and conquereth.

Farewell, the sovereign of all virtue and goddess of all virgins, Diana, whose perfections are impossible to be number'd and therefore infinite, never to be matched and therefore immortal. Farewell sweet parents, yet, to be mine, unfortunate parents. How blessed had you been in barrenness, how happy had I been if I had not been! Farewell life, vain life, wretched life, whose sorrows are long, whose end doubtful, whose miseries certain, whose hopes innumerable, whose fears intolerable. Come, death, and welcome, death, whom nature cannot resist, because necessity ruleth, nor defer, because destiny hasteth. Come, Agar, thou unsatiable monster of maidens' blood and devourer of beauties' bowels, glut thyself till thou surfeit, and let my life end thine. Tear these tender joints with thy greedy jaws, these yellow locks with thy black feet, this fair face with thy foul teeth. Why abatest thou thy wonted swiftness? I am fair, I am a virgin, I am ready. Come, Agar, thou horrible monster, and farewell world, thou viler monster.

Gorboduc

Thomas Sackville and Thomas Norton
1561

Scene: legendary England

Female—Dramatic
  Videna: Queen of Britain, 40–50

> When her beloved son, Ferrex, is murdered by his brother, the grieving queen vows
> to avenge his death.

VIDENA: Why should I live and linger forth my time
In longer life to double my distress?
O me, most woeful wight, whom no mishap
Long ere this day could have bereaved hence.
Mought[47] not these hands, by fortune or by fate,
Have pierced this breast and life with iron reft?
Or in this palace here, where I so long
Have spent my days, could not that happy hour
Once, once have happed in which these hugy frames
With death by fall might have oppressed me?[48]
Or should not this most hard and cruel soil,
So oft where I have pressed my wretched steps,
Sometime had ruth[49] of mine accursed life
To rend in twain and swallow me therein?
So had my bones possessed now in peace
Their happy grave within the closed ground,
And greedy worms had gnawn his pined[50] heart
Without my feeling pain: so should not now
This living breast remain the ruthful tomb,
Wherein my heart yelden[51] to death is graved;[52]
Nor dreary thoughts, with pangs of pining grief,
My doleful mind had not afflicted thus.

---

[47]might
[48]"Why could not this palace have fallen on me and brought death before this hour?"
[49]pity
[50]Wasted, suffering.
[51]yielded
[52]buried

O my beloved son! O my sweet child!
My dear Ferrex, my joy, my life's delight!
Is my beloved son, is my sweet child,
My dear Ferrex, my joy, my life's delight,[53]
Murdered with cruel death? O hateful wretch!
O heinous traitor both to heaven and earth!
Thou, Porrex, thou this damned deed has wrought;
Thou, Porrex, thou shalt dearly 'bye[54] the same.
Traitor to kin and kind, to sire and me,
To thine own flesh, and traitor to thyself,
The gods on thee in hell shall wreak their wrath,
And here in earth this hand shall take revenge
On thee, Porrex, thou false and caitiff wight.[55]
If after blood so eager were thy thirst
And murderous mind had so possessed thee,
If such hard heart of rock and stony flint
Lived in thy breast that nothing else could like[56]
Thy cruel tyrant's thought but death and blood,
Wild savage beasts, mought not their slaughter serve
To feed thy greedy will, and in the midst
Of their entrails to stain thy deadly hands
With blood deserved and drink thereof thy fill?
Or if naught else but death and blood of man
Mought please thy lust, could none in Britain Land.
Whose heart betorn out of his panting breast
With thine own hand, or work what death thou wouldst,
Suffice to make a sacrifice to 'pease
That deadly mind and murderous thought in thee,
But he who in the selfsame womb was wrapped,
Where thou in dismal hour receivedst life?
Or if needs thy hand must slaughter make,
Moughtest thou not have reached a mortal wound,
And with thy sword have pierced this cursed womb

---

[53]The line may be a compositorial repetition of line 24 just above.
[54]atone for
[55]Treacherous creature.
[56]satisfy

That the accursed Porrex brought to light,
And given me a just reward therefor?
So Ferrex yet sweet life mought have enjoyed,
And to his aged father comfort brought
With some young son in whom they both might live.
But whereunto waste I this ruthful speech,
To thee that hast thy brother's blood thus shed?
Shall I still think that from this womb thou sprung?
That I thee bare? Or take thee for my son?
No, traitor, no; I thee refuse for mine!
Murderer, I thee renounce; thou art not mine.
Never, O wretch, this womb conceived thee,
No never bode[57] I painful throes for thee.
Changeling[58] to me thou art, and not my child,
Nor to no wight that spark of pity knew.
Ruthless, unkind, monster of nature's work,
Thou never sucked the milk of woman's breast,
But from thy birth the cruel tiger's teats
Have nursed thee; nor yet of flesh and blood
Formed is thy heart, but of hard iron wrought;
And wild and desert woods bred thee to life.[59]
But canst thou hope to 'scape my just revenge,
Or that these hands will not be wroke[60] on thee?
Dost thou not know that Ferrex' mother lives,
That loved him more dearly than herself?
And doth she live and is not venged on thee?

---

[57]Endured, bore.
[58]A child secretly put in the place of another.
[59]cf. Virgil *Aeneid* iv. 365–367 and Seneca *Hercules Oetaeus*, 11. 143–146 (Walsh).
[60]avenged

Hey for Honesty

Thomas Randolph

1651

Scene: mythic Britain

Female—Serio-comic
> Anus: a disgruntled woman, 40–50

Here, the aging Anus bemoans the fact that men seem to prefer younger women.

ANUS: Heigho! methinks I am sick with lying alone last night. Well, I will scratch out the eyes of this same rascally Plutus, god of wealth, that has undone me. Alas! poor woman, since the shop of Plutus his eyes has been open, what abundance of misery has befallen thee! Now the young gallant will no longer kiss thee nor embrace thee; but thou, poor widow, must lie comfortless in a solitary pair of sheets, having nothing to cover thee but the lecherous rug and the bawdy blankets. O, that I were young again! how it comforts me to remember the death of my maidenhead! Alas! poor woman, they contemn old age, as if our lechery was out of date. They say we are cold: methinks that thought should make 'um take compassion of us, and lie with us—if not for love, for charity. They say we are dry: so much the more capable of Cupid's fire; while young wenches, like green wood, smoke before they flame. They say we are old: why, then, experience makes us more expert. They tell us our lips are wrinkled: why that in kissing makes the sweeter titillation. They swear we have no teeth: why, then, they need not fear biting. Well, if our lease of lechery be out, yet methinks we might purchase a night-labourer for his day's wages. I will be revenged of this same Plutus, that wrongs the orphans, and is so uncharitable to the widows.

The Lady of Pleasure

James Shirley
1635

Scene: the Strand

Female—Serio-comic
   Celestina: a wealthy young widow, 18–25

   Here, the crafty young widow reveals her secret for attracting men.

CELESTINA: One thing I'll tell you more, and this I give you
Worthy of your imitation from my practice:
You see me merry, full of song and dancing,
Pleasant in language, apt to all delights
That crown a public meeting, but you cannot
Accuse me of being prodigal of my favours
To any of my guests. I do not summon
(By any wink) a gentleman to follow me
To my withdrawing chamber; I hear all
Their pleas in court;[61] nor can they boast abroad
(And do me justice) after a salute
They have much conversation with my lip.
I hold the kissing of my hand a courtesy,
And he that loves me must, upon the strength
Of that, expect[62] till I renew his favour.
Some ladies are so expensive[63] in their graces
To those that honour 'em, and so prodigal,
That in a little time they have nothing but
The naked sin left to reward their servants;
Whereas a thrift in our rewards will keep
Men long in their devotion, and preserve
Our selves in stock,[64] to encourage those that honour us.
[ISABELLA: This is an art worthy of a lady's practice.]

---

[61]publicly
[62]wait
[63]Eager to expend, lavish.
[64]Literally "possessed of capital" in keeping with the metaphor of "prodigal" expenditure in the preceeding lines.

CELESTINA: It takes not from the freedom of our mirth,
But seems to advance it, when we can possess
Our pleasures with security of our honour;
And that preserved, I welcome all the joys
My fancy[65] can let in. In this I have given
The copy[66] of my mind, nor do I blush
You understand it.

---

[65]Amorous inclination.
[66]Possibly a pun: (1) fullness, abundance, copiousness; (2) the pattern or original from which copies can be made.

Lena

Ludovicio Ariosto
1528

Scene: Ferrara

Female—Serio-Comic
   Lena: a high-strung and selfish woman, 20–30

Married Lena has been having an affair with Fazio. When the lovers quarrel over
money, Fazio sees an opportunity to end things. Here, Lena rages against being
dumped by her lover.

LENA: (Soliloquizing.) My god, he does want things all his own way!
He thinks he can poison me with his stinking breath, ride me to exhaus-
tion like a damned donkey, and then reward me with a "Thank you
very much!" A fine young gallant he is, to make a girl want to give him
something for nothing! Oh! I was a silly woman to listen to his stories
and his promises in the first place. But my useless brute of a husband
kept on at me about it, till I thought he'd never stop. "My dear, you'd
better do what he wants. It'll make our fortune! If you know how to
handle him, he'll pay all our debts." And anyone would have believed
it to begin with. He promised us the earth and all that therein is, as
these scholars say. Well, he laid a trap for us, and I hope to see him
break his own neck in it. Since he won't keep all those promises, I'm
going to behave like servants do when their wages aren't paid—they
get their own back on their masters by cheating them, robbing them
and murdering them. And I'm going to get paid somehow, too, and I'll
do anything, whether it's right or wrong. And no one can blame me for
it—neither god nor man. If Fazio had a wife, I'd put all my efforts into
making him a . . . . , a . . . . —what he's made Pacifico. But that's impossible, because his wife's dead; so I'll make him a . . . . —what I said
before—through his daughter.

The Life and Death of King John

William Shakespeare

1595

Scene: France

Female—Dramatic
Constance: mother of the Duke of Brittany, 40s

Constance is incensed that England should be ruled by the weak and foolish John and pushes her son, Arthur, to claim the British throne for France. Here, she demands that Arthur press his suit.

CONSTANCE: If thou, that bid'st me be content, wert grim,
Ugly and slanderous to thy mother's womb,
Full of unpleasing blots and sightless stains,
Lame, foolish, crooked, swart, prodigious,
Patch'd with foul moles and eye-offending marks,
I would not care, I then would be content,
For then I should not love thee, no, nor thou
Become thy great birth nor deserve a crown.
But thou art fair, and at thy birth, dear boy.
Nature and Fortune join'd to make thee great:
Of Nature's gifts thou mayst with lilies boast
And with the half-blown rose. But Fortune, O,
She is corrupted, changed and won from thee;
She adulterates hourly with thine uncle John,
And with her golden hand hath pluck'd on France
To tread down fair respect of sovereignty,
And made his majesty the bawd to theirs.
France is a bawd to Fortune and King John,
That strumpet Fortune, that usurping John!
Tell me, thou fellow, is not France forsworn?
Envenom him with words, or get thee gone
And leave those woes alone which I alone
Am bound to under-bear.
[SALISBURY: Pardon me, madam,
I may not go without you to the kings.]
CONSTANCE: Thou mayst, thou shalt; I will not go with thee:

I will instruct my sorrows to be proud;
For grief is proud and makes his owner stoop.
To me and to the slate of my great grief
Let kings assemble; for my grief's so great
That no supporter but the huge firm earth
Can hold it up: here I and sorrows sit;
Here is my throne, bid kings come bow to it.
(*Seats herself on the ground.*)

The Longer Thou Livest

W. Wager
1569

Scene: non-specific

Female—Dramatic
    Fortune: the eternal Mistress of Fate, any age

> As Wrath, Discipline and Idleness discuss their sovereignty over a simple foolish
> man, Fortune appears and reminds them that she is ruler over all.[67]

FORTUNE: No God's mercy? no reverence? no honor?
No cap off? no knee bowed? no homage?
Who am I? is there no more good manner?
I trow, you know me not nor my lineage.
I tell you, I rule and govern all;
I advance and I pluck down again;
Of him that of birth is poor and small
As a noble man I can make to reign;
I am she that may do all things.
In heaven or earth who is like to me?
I make captives of lords and kings,
Of captives or fools I make kings to be.
No curtsey yet for all this power?
I tell you learned men call me a goddess.
A beggar I make rich in an hour;
To such as I love, I give good success.
Who in this world can me withstand?
Who can say yea, where I say nay?
I change all in the turning of a hand;
Whatsoever I will do, do it I may.
Have I done nothing for any here?
Have I not one lover nor friend?
None to welcome me with a merry cheer?
Now by my truth you be unkind.
Well, I may chance some to displease,

---

[67]Fortune probably carries her symbolic wheel; it is doubtful, however, that she is blind-folded, since she comments that the audience has not paid her proper homage.

I purpose to dally and play a feat
Which shall turn some to small ease;
A popish fool will I place in a wiseman's seat.
By that you shall learn, I trow,
To do your duty to a lady so high;
He shall teach you Fortune to know
And to honor her till you die.

A Looking Glass for London and England

Thomas Lodge and Robert Greene
@1600

Scene: Assyria

Female—Serio-Comic
Remilia: Princess of Assyria; hopelessly vain, 20s

> Here, this foolishly self-centered young woman encourages her ladies-in-waiting to praise her beauty.

REMILIA: Fair Queens, yet handmaids unto Rasni's love,
Tell me, is not my state as glorious
As Juno's pomp when, 'tired with heaven's despoil,
Clad in her vestments, spotted all with stars,
She crossed the silver path unto her Jove?
Is not Remilia far more beauteous,
Riched with the pride of nature's excellence,
Than Venus in the brightest of her shine?
My hairs, surpass they not Apollo's locks?
Are not my tresses curlèd with such art
As love delights to hide him in their fair?
Doth not mine eye shine like the morning lamp
That tells Aurora[68] when her love will come?
Have I not stol'n the beauty of the heavens
And placed it on the feature of my face?
Can any goddess make compare with me,
Or match her with the fair Remilia?
[ALVIDA: The beauties that proud Paris saw from Troy,
Must'ring in Ida for the golden ball,[69]
Were not so gorgeous as Remilia.]
REMILIA: I have tricked my trammels[70] up with the richest balm,
And made my perfumes of the purest myrrh.

---

[68]Goddess of the dawn.
[69]Paris presided over a beauty contest on Mount Ida among Hera (Juno), Aphrodite (Venus), and Athena (Minerva) for the prize of a golden apple.
[70]Plaits, braids, fishing nets.

The precious drugs that Egypt's wealth affords,
The costly paintings fetched from curious[71] Tyre,
Have mended in my face what nature missed.
Am I not the earth's wonder in my looks?
[ALVIDA: Madam, unless you coy it[72] trick and trim,[73]
And play the civil wanton[74] ere you yield,
Smiting disdain of pleasures with your tongue,
Patting your princely Rasni on the cheek
When he presumes to kiss without consent,
You mar the market. Beauty naught avails;
You must be proud, for pleasures hardly[75] got
Are sweet if once attained.]
REMILIA: Fair Alvida,
Thy counsel makes Remilia passing wise.
Suppose that thou wert Rasni's mightiness,
And I, Remilia, prince of excellence.
[ALVIDA: I would be master then of love and thee.]
REMILIA: Of love and me. Proud and disdainful King,
Dar'st thou presume to touch a deity
Before she grace thee with a yielding smile?
[ALVIDA: Tut, my Remilia, be not thou so coy;
Say nay and take it.]
REMILIA: Careless and unkind,[76]
Talks Rasni to Remilia in such sort
As if I did enjoy a human form?
Look on thy love, behold mine eyes divine;
And dar'st thou twit me with a woman's fault?
Ah, Rasni, thou art rash to judge of me.
I tell thee Flora oft hath wooed my lips
To lend a rose to beautify her spring;
The sea-nymphs fetch their lilies from my cheeks.
Then thou unkind, and hereon would I weep.

. . . .

[71]Ingenious, artistic.
[72]Act coyly.
[73]Neatly, elegantly.
[74]Behave with restrained lewdness.
[75]With difficulty.
[76]unnatural

[*ALVIDA:* And here would Alvida resign her charge,
For were I but in thought th' Assyrian King,
I needs must quite[77] thy tears with kisses sweet,
And crave a pardon with a friendly touch.
You know it, madam, though I teach it not—
The touch, I mean; you smile when as you think it.]
REMILIA: How am I pleased to hear thy pretty prate
According to the humor of my mind.
Ah, nymphs, who fairer than Remilia?
The gentle winds have wooed me with their sighs,
The frowning air hath cleared when I did smile;
And when I traced[78] upon the tender grass,
Love, that makes warm the center of the earth,
Lift up his crest to kiss Remilia's foot.
Juno still entertains her amorous Jove
With new delights for fear he look on me;
The phoenix'[79] feathers are become my fan,
For I am beauty's phoenix in this world.
Shut close these curtains straight and shadow me
For fear Apollo spy me in his walks,
And scorn all eyes to see Remilia's eyes.
Nymphs, eunuchs, sing, for Mavors draweth nigh.
Hide me in closure, let him long to look,
For were a goddess fairer than am I,
I'll scale the heavens to pull her from the place.

---

[77]stop
[78]Passed, trod.
[79]The phoenix was a legendary bird, the only one of its kind, said to live hundreds of years, burn itself on a funeral pyre, and rise from its ashes to live another cycle.

A Mad World, My Masters

Thomas Middleton

1606

Scene: London

#1 Female—Dramatic
>   Mother: a coarse and scheming woman, 40–50

>   Here, the mother of a well-used courtesan reveals her plans for the girl's future.

MOTHER: Every part of the world shoots up daily into more subtlety.
The very spider weaves her cauls[80] with more art and cunning to
>   entrap the fly.
The shallow plowman can distinguish now
'Twixt simple truth and a dissembling brow,
Your base mechanic[81] fellow can spy out
A weakness in a lord, and learns to flout.
How does't behoove us then that live by sleight
To have our wits wound up to their stretch'd height!
Fifteen times thou know'st I have sold thy maidenhead
To make up a dowry for thy marriage, and yet
There's maidenhead enough for old Sir Bounteous still.
He'll be all his lifetime about it yet,
And be as far to seek when he has done.
The sums that I have told upon thy pillow!
I shall once see those golden days again;
Though fifteen, all thy maidenheads are not gone.
The Italian is not serv'd yet, nor the French;
The British men come for a dozen at once,
They engross all the market. Tut, my girl,
'Tis nothing but a politic conveyance,[82]
A sincere carriage, a religious eyebrow
That throws their charms over the worldings' senses;
And when thou spiest a fool that truly pities
The false springs of thine eyes,

---

[80]spider webs
[81]laboring
[82]Behavior, with a sense of "cunning, trickery."

And honorably dotes upon thy love,
If he be rich, set him by for a husband.
Be wisely tempered and learn this, my wench,
Who gets th' opinion[83] for a virtuous name
May sin at pleasure, and ne'er think of shame.

#2 Female—Serio-Comic
Courtesan: a well-used woman, 20–30

Here, the brassy courtesan tells another woman how to best make her husband
jealous.

COURTESAN: When husbands in their rank'st suspicions dwell,
Then 'tis our best art to dissemble well.
Put but these notes in use that I'll direct you
He'll curse himself that e'er he did suspect you.
Perhaps he will solicit you, as in trial,
To visit such and such: still give denial.
Let no persuasions sway you; they are but fetches
Set to betray you, jealousies, slights, and reaches.
Seem in his sight to endure the sight of no man;
Put by all kisses, till you kiss in common;
Neglect all entertain; if he bring in
Strangers, keep you your chamber, be not seen;
If he chance steal upon you, let him find
Some book lie open 'gainst an unchaste mind,
And coted[84] scriptures, though for your own pleasure
You read some stirring pamphlet, and convey it
Under your skirt, the fittest place to lay it.
This is the course, my wench, to enjoy thy wishes;
Here you perform best when you most neglect;
The way to daunt is to outvie suspect.[85]
Manage these principles but with art and life,
Welcome all nations, thou'rt an honest wife.

....

[83]reputation
[84]quoted
[85]suspicion

The Maid's Tragedy

Beaumont and Fletcher
1611

Scene: The city of Rhodes

#1 Female—Dramatic
   Evadne: a woman holding a terrible secret, 20s

The King of Rhodes has forced young Amnitor to renounce his beloved Aspatia to marry Evadne, the king's secret mistress. On their wedding night, Evadne confesses her affair with the king to Amnitor and begs his forgiveness.

EVADNE: My lord,
Give me your griefs: You are an innocent,
A soul as white as heaven; let not my sins
Perish your noble youth. I do not fall here
To shadow, by dissembling with my tears,
(As, all say, women can), or to make less,
What my hot will hath done, which Heaven and you
Know to be tougher than the hand of time
Can cut from man's remembrance. No, I do not:
I do appear the same, the same Evadne,
Drest in the shames I lived in: the same monster!
But these are names of honour, to what I am:
I do present myself the foulest creature,
Most poisonous, dangerous, and despised of men,
Lerna e'er bred, or Nilus! I am hell,
Till you, my dear lord, shoot your light into me,
The beams of your forgiveness. I am soulsick,
And wither with the fear of one condemn'd,
Till I have got your pardon.

#2 Female—Dramatic
   Evadne

When her hot-headed brother discovers the truth about her relationship with the king, he demands that Evadne murder her lover in the name of righteousness. Here, Evadne approaches the sleeping king and prepares to carry out her brother's wishes.

EVADNE: The night grows horrible; and all about me
Like my black purpose. Oh, the conscience

Of a lost virgin! whither wilt thou pull me?
To what things, dismal as the depth of hell,
Wilt thou provoke me? Let no woman dare
From this hour be disloyal, if her heart be flesh,
If she have blood, and can fear: 'Tis a daring
Above that desperate fool's that left his peace,
And went to sea to fight. 'Tis so many sins,
An age cannot repent 'em; and so great,
The gods want mercy for! Yet I must through 'em.
I have begun a slaughter on my honour,
And I must end it there.— He sleeps. Good Heavens!
Why give you peace to this untemperate beast,
That hath so long transgress'd you; I must kill him,
And I will do it bravely: The mere joy
Tells me, I merit in it. Yet I must not
Thus tamely do it, as he sleeps; that were
To rock him to another world: My vengeance
Shall take him waking, and then lay before him
The number of his wrongs and punishments.
I'll shake his sins like furies, till I waken His evil angel, his sick
    conscience;
And then I'll strike him dead. King, by your leave: (*Ties his arms to the
    bed.*)
I dare not trust your strength. Your grace and I
Must grapple upon even terms no more.
So. If he rail me not from my resolution,
I shall be strong enough.— My lord the king!!

The Masque of Queens

Ben Jonson
1609

Scene: the meeting of a witches coven

Female—Serio-Comic
   Hag: a witch, any age

   Here, a lowly witch reports on her nefarious activities to a superior.

HAG: I have been all day looking after
A raven, feeding upon a quarter;[86]
And soon as she turned her beak to the south,
I snatched this morsel out of her mouth.

I have been gathering wolves' hairs,
The mad dog's foam, and the adder's ears,
The spurging[87] of a dead man's eyes,
And all since the evening star did rise.

I last night lay all alone
On the ground, to hear the Mandrake[88] groan,
And plucked him up, though he grew full low,
And as I had done, the cock did crow.

And I have been choosing out this skull
From charnel-houses[89] that were full,
From private grots, and public pits,
And frighted sexton[90] out of his wits.

....

[86]At a time when drawing and quartering were often part of an execution, the nature of the
quarter would be evident.
[87]oozing
[88]A dangerous aphrodisiac, a root with a human voice which was death to hear.
[89]Houses for storing old dead bones.
[90]Guardian of a graveyard.

Under a cradle I did creep
By day; and when the child was asleep,
At night I sucked the breath; and rose,
And plucked the nodding nurse by the nose.

I had a dagger, what did I with that?
Killed an infant to have his fat.
A piper it got, at a church ale,[91]
I bade him again blow wind in the tail.

A murderer yon was hung in chains,
The sun and the wind had shrunk his veins;
I bit off a sinew, I clipped his hair,
I brought off his rags that danced in the air.

The screech-owl's eggs and the feathers black,
The blood of the frog and the bone in his back,
I have been getting, and made of his skin
A purset, to keep Sir Cranion in.[92]

And I have been plucking, plants among,
Hemlock, henbane, adder's tongue,
Nightshade, moonwort, leopard's bane,[93]
And twice by the dogs was like to be ta'en.

I from the jaws of a gardener's bitch
Did snatch these bones, and then leaped the ditch,
Yet went I back to the house again,
Killed the black cat—and here's the brain.

I went to the toad breeds under the wall,
I charmed him out, and he came at my call;
I scratched out the eyes of the owl, before;
I tore the bat's wing; what would you have more?

[91]Church-ales were church-festivals, often quite alcoholic. To "blow wind in the tail" is a vague but clearly contemptuous expression.
[92]Her familiar spirit, perhaps in the form of a spider.
[93]These are all vegetables of evil omen.

The Merry Wives of Windsor
William Shakespeare
1598

Scene: Windsor

#1 Female—Serio-Comic
        Mrs. Page: a virtuous wife, 30s

> When Mrs. Page receives a love letter from the rascally John Falstaff, she vows to revenge herself of his impudence.

MRS. PAGE: What, have I scaped love-letters in the holiday-time of my beauty, and am I now a subject for them? Let me see. (*Reads.*)

"Ask me no reason why I love you; for though Love use Reason for his physician, he admits him not for his counsellor. You are not young, no more am I; go to then, there's sympathy: you are merry, so am I; ha, ha! then there's more sympathy: you love sack, and so do I; would you desire better sympathy? Let it suffice thee, Mistress Page,—at the least, if the love of soldier can suffice,—that I love thee. I will not say, pity me; 'tis not a soldier-like phrase: but I say, love me. By me,

Thine own true knight,

By day or night,

Or any kind of light,

With all his might

For thee to fight,   JOHN FALSTAFF."

What a Herod of Jewry is this! O wicked, wicked world! One that is well-nigh worn to pieces with age to show himself a young gallant! What an unweighed behaviour hath this Flemish drunkard picked— with the devil's name!—out of my conversation, that he dares in this manner assay me? Why, he hath not been thrice in my company! What should I say to him? I was then frugal of my mirth: Heaven forgive me! Why, I'll exhibit a bill in the parliament for the putting down of men. How shall I be revenged on him? for revenged I will be, as sure as his guts are made of puddings.

No Wit, No Help Like a Woman's

Thomas Middleton
1613

Scene: London

#1 Female—Dramatic
    Mistress Low-Water: a woman struggling with ethical questions, 30–40

> Mistress Low-Water would very much like to improve her material lot in life. Here, she agonizes over her lack of legitimate options.

MISTRESS LOW-WATER: Is there no saving-means? No help religious
For a distressed gentlewoman to live by?
Has virtue no renevue?[94] Who has all then?
Is the world's lease from hell, the devil head-landlord?
Oh, how was conscience, the right heir, put by?
Law would not do such an unrighteous deed,
Though with the fall of angels 't had been fee'd.
Where are our hopes in banks? Was honesty
A younger sister without portion left?
No dowry in the Chamber[95] beside wantonness?
O miserable orphan!
'Twixt two extremes runs there no blessed mean,
No comfortable strain[96] that a I may kiss it?
Must I to whoredom, or to beggary lean,
My mind being sound? Is there no way to miss it?
Is't not injustice that a widow laughs
And lays her mourning part upon a wife?
That she should have the garment, I the heart;
My wealth her uncle[97] left her, and me her grief?
Yet, stood all miseries in their loathed'st forms

---

[94]This phrase and others in the speech are similar to those in *The Revenger's Tragedy*, II.i.1–8, a play often attributed to Middleton.

[95]The treasury of the City of London, in which orphans' inheritances were deposited until they came of age. Middleton and his sister, Avis, received their inheritance from the Chamber (see Mark Eccles, "Thomas Middleton a Poett," *Studies in Philology* 54 [1957]: 517).

[96]Harmonious melody.

[97]Should read "husband," but Middleton failed to change the relationship from the source play's "uncle."

On this hand of me, thick like a foul mist,
And here the bright enticements of the world
In clearest colors, flattery, and advancement,
And all the bastard glories this frame jets in,[98]
Horror nor splendor, shadows fair nor foul
Should force me shame my husband, wound my soul.

---

[98]this world struts in

Perkin Warbeck

John Ford
1634

Scene: Ireland

Female—Dramatic
Lady Katherine Gordon: a woman in exile, 20–30

Katherine is a woman of noble Scottish birth married to Perkin Warbeck, a scheming pretender to the throne of Henry VII. Warbeck's claim is backed by James IV of Scotland. Eventually, a treaty between James and Henry results in Warbeck and Katherine's exile to Ireland. Here, the homesick Scot shares a lonely moment with her maid.

KATHERINE: It is decreed; and we must yield to fate,
Whose angry justice, though it threaten ruin,
Contempt, and poverty, is all but trial
Of a weak woman's constancy in suffering.
Here in a stranger's and an enemy's land,
Forsaken and unfurnish'd of all hopes
But such as wait on misery, I range
To meet affliction wheresoe'er I tread.
My train and pomp of servants is reduc'd
To one kind gentlewoman and this groom.
Sweet Jane, now whither must we?
[*JANE:* To your ships, Dear lady, and turn home.]
KATHERINE: Home! I have none,
Fly thou to Scotland, thou hast friends will weep
For joy to bid thee welcome, But oh Jane,
My Jane, my friends are desperate[99] of comfort
As I must be of them; the common charity,
Good people's alms, and prayers of the gentle
Is the revenue must support my state.
As for my native country, since it once
Saw me a princess in the height of greatness
My birth allow'd me, here I make a vow
Scotland shall never see me, being fallen

....

[99]without hope

Or lessened in my fortunes. Never, Jane,
Never to Scotland more will I return.
Could I be England's queen (a glory, Jane,
I never fawn'd on), yet the king who gave me
Hath sent me with my husband from his presence,
Deliver'd us suspected to his nation,
Render'd us spectacles to time and pity.
And it is fit I should return to such
As only listen after our descent
From happiness enjoy'd to misery
Expected, though uncertain? Never, never!
Alas, why dost thou weep, and that poor creature
Wipe his wet cheeks too? Let me feel alone
Extremities, who know to give them harbor.
Nor thou nor he has cause. You may live safely.

The Sad Shepherd

Ben Jonson

1604

Scene: the Sherwood of Robin Hood

Female—Serio-Comic
> Amie: an innocent young shepherdess, 16–18

> Amie has fallen in love, but is ignorant of the cause of this strange new malaise. Here, the unhappy young woman describes her "symptoms" to Maid Marian.

AMIE: No, Marian, my disease is somewhat nigher.
I weep, and boil away myself in tears;
And then my panting heart would dry those fears.
I burn, though all the forest lend a shade,
And freeze, though the whole wood one fire were made.[100]
[*MARIAN*: Alas!]
AMIE: I often have been torn with thorn and brier,
Both in the leg and foot, and somewhat higher,
Yet gave not then such fearful shrieks as these. Ah!
I often have been stung too with curst[101] bees,
Yet not remember that I then did quit
Either my company or mirth for it. Ah!
And therefore what it is that I feel now,
And know no cause of it, nor where, nor how
It entered in me, nor least print can see,
I feel, afflicts me more than brier or bee. O!
How often when the sun, heaven's brightest birth,
Hath with his burning fervor cleft the earth,
Under a spreading elm or oak hard by
A cool, clear fountain could I sleeping lie,
Safe from the heat! But now no shady tree
Nor purling brook can my refreshing be.
Oft when the meadows were grown rough with frost,
The rivers ice-bound, and their currents lost,

---

[100]Amie's disease has all the traditional symptoms and traditional rhetoric of Petrarchan love.
[101]Mischievous, malicious.

My thick, warm fleece I wore was my defense;
Or large, good fires I made drave[102] winter thence.
But now my whole flock's fells[103] nor this thick grove,
Enflamed to ashes, can my cold remove.
It is a cold and heat that doth outgo
All sense of winter's and of summer's so.

---

[102]drove
[103]I.e., neither all the wool of my flock, nor all the wood of the forest if it were burned, could remove my cold.

The Spanish Tragedy

Thomas Kyd

1584–89

#3 Female—Dramatic
> Bel-Imperia: a woman grieving for the death of her love, 20s

> Bel-Imperia's lover, Horatio, has been murdered by the Prince of Portugal and his accomplices. Here, the grief-stricken young woman goads Horatio's father, Hieronimo, into seeking justice for his son's death.

BEL-IMPERIA: Is this the love thou bear'st Horatio?
Is this the kindness that thou counterfeits?
Are these the fruits of thine incessant tears?
Hieronimo, are these thy passions,
Thy protestations and thy deep laments
That thou were wont[104] to weary men withal?
O unkind father! O deceitful world!
With what excuses canst thou show thyself
From this dishonor and the hate of men,
Thus to neglect the loss of life and of him
Whom both my letters and thine own belief
Assures thee to be causeless slaughterèd?
Hieronimo, for shame, Hieronimo,
Be not a history to after times
Of such ingratitude unto thy son.
Unhappy mothers of such children then,
But monstrous fathers to forget so soon
The death of those whom they with care and cost
Have tendered so, thus careless should be lost.
Myself, a stranger in respect of thee,
So loved his life as still I wish their deaths.
Nor shall his death be unrevenged by me,
Although I bear it out for fashion's sake.[105]
For here I swear, in sight of heaven and earth,
Shouldst thou neglect the love thou shouldst retain,

---

[104]accustomed
[105]That is, pretend to accept the situation

And give it over and devise no more,
Myself should send their hateful souls to hell
That wrought his downfall with extremest death.

#4 Female—Dramatic
Isabella: a woman driven to suicide by the death of her son, 40–50

When Isabella is told that her beloved son, Horatio, has been murdered, she goes to the arbor where the killers hung his body and destroys it just before taking her own life.

ISABELLA: Tell me no more!—O monstrous homicides!
Since neither piety nor pity moves
The King to justice or compassion,
I will revenge myself upon this place,
Where thus they murdered my belovèd son.
(*She cuts down the arbor.*)
Down with these branches and these loathsome boughs
Of this unfortunate and fatal pine.
Down with them, Isabella; rent[106] them up,
And burn the roots from whence the rest is sprung.
I will not leave a root, a stalk, a tree,
A bough, a branch, a blossom, nor a leaf,
No, not an herb within this garden plot,
Accursèd complot[107] of my misery.
Fruitless for ever may this garden be,
Barren the earth, and blissless whosoever
Imagines not to keep it unmanured.[108]
An eastern wind, commixed with noisome airs,
Shall blast the plants and the young saplings;
The earth with serpents shall be pesterèd,
And passengers,[109] for fear to be infect,
Shall stand aloof, and, looking at it, tell:
"There, murdered, died the son of Isabel."
Ay, here he died, and here I him embrace.

[106]rend
[107]accomplice
[108]uncultivated
[109]passers-by

See, where his ghost solicits with his wounds
Revenge on her that should revenge his death.
Hieronimo, make haste to see thy son,
For sorrow and despair hath cited[110] me
To hear Horatio plead with Rhadamanth.
Make haste, Hieronimo, to hold excused
Thy negligence in pursuit of their deaths
Whose hateful wrath bereaved him of his breath.
Ah, nay, thou dost delay their deaths,
Forgives the murderers of thy noble son,
And none but I bestir me—to no end.
And as I curse this tree from further fruit,
So shall my womb be cursèd for his sake;
And with this weapon will I wound the breast,
The hapless breast that gave Horatio suck.
(*She stabs herself.*)

---

[110]summoned

Summer's Last Will and Testament

Thomas Nashe

1592

Scene: the changing of the seasons

#1 Female—Serio-Comic
   Winter: the spirit of the cold dark months, 30–60

As Summer prepares to pass his crown to Autumn, the seasons squabble amongst themselves. Here, Winter delivers a damning speech in which she reveals her contempt for those who admire the other seasons.

WINTER: Then, duty laid aside, you do me wrong.
I am more worthy of it far than he:
He hath no skill nor courage for to rule.
A weather-beaten bankrupt ass it is,
That scatters and consumeth all he hath:
Each one do pluck from him without control.
He is nor hot nor cold; a silly soul,
That fain would please each party, if so he might.
He and the Spring are scholar's favorites;
What scholars are, what thriftless kind of men,
Yourself be judge, and judge of him by them.
When Cerberus[111] was headlong drawn from hell,
He voided a black poison from his mouth
Called *Aconitum*,[112] whereof ink was made.
That ink, with reeds first laid on dried barks,
Served men a while to make rude works withal,
Till Hermes, secretary to the gods,
Or Hermes Trismegistus,[113] as some will,
Weary with graving in blind[114] characters,
And figures of familiar beasts and plants,
Invented letters to write lies withal.

---

[111]Monstrous dog that guarded the entrance to the Underworld, dragged away by Hercules.

[112]Poisonous plant, monkshood or wolfsbane.

[113]Legendary magician, king, priest, prophet, and sophist, credited in the Renaissance with the authorship of a vast body of occult writings and often identified with the Greek god Hermes.

[114]obscure

In them he penned the fables of the gods,
The giants' war, and thousand tales besides.
After each nation got these toys in use
There grew up certain drunken parasites,[115]
Termed poets, which, for a meal's meat or two,
Would promise monarchs immortality.
They vomited in verse all that they knew;
Found causes and beginnings of the world;
Fetched pedigrees of mountains and of floods,
From men and women whom the gods transformed.
If any town or city they passed by
Had in compassion, thinking them mad men,
Forborne to whip them or imprison them,
That city was not built by human hands;
'Twas raised by music, like Megara[116] walls;
Apollo, poets' patron, founded it,
Because they found one fitting favor there.
Musaeus,[117] Linus,[118] Homer, Orpheus,
Were of this trade, and thereby won their fame.
[WILL S: *Fama malum, quo non velocius ullum.*[119]]
WINTER: Next them a company of ragged knaves,
Sun-bathing beggars, lazy hedge-creepers,
Sleeping face upwards in the fields all night,
Dreamed strange devices of the sun and moon;
And they, like gypsies, wandering up and down,
Told fortunes, juggled, nicknamed all the stars,
And were of idiots termed philosophers.
Such was Pythagoras, the silencer;[120]
Prometheus,[121] Thales, Milesius,[122]
Who would all things of water should be made:

---

[115]Men who flatter in order to cadge meals.
[116]Corinthian city.
[117]Mythical singer.
[118]legendary
[119]L.: Fame, swiftest of all evils; misquoted from *Aeneid*, IV. 474.
[120]Novices in the school of Pythagoras were committed to a long period of silence.
[121]Demigod who stole fire from heaven.
[122]Thales of Miletus, one of the Seven Sages, Greek philosopher and scientist, sixth century B.C.

Anaximander,[123] Anaxamines,[124]

That positively said the air was god:

Xenocrates,[125] that said there were eight gods;

And Cratoniates, Alcmeon[126] too,

Who thought the sun and moon and stars were gods.

The poorer sort of them, that could get nought,

Professed, like beggarly Franciscan friars,

And the strict order of the Capuchins,

A voluntary, wretched poverty,

Contempt of gold, thin fare, and lying hard.

Yet he that was most vehement in these,

Diogenes[127] the cynic and the dog,

Was taken coining money in his cell.

[*WILL S:* What an old ass was that. Methinks he should have coined
carrot-roots rather; for, as for money he had no use for 't except it were
to melt, and solder up holes in his tub withal.]

WINTER: It were a whole Olympiad's[128] work to tell

How many devilish, *ergo*, armèd arts,

Sprung all as vices of this idleness:

For even as soldiers not employed in wars,

But living loosely in a quiet state,

Not having wherewithal to maintain pride,

Nay, scarce to find their bellies any food,

Nought but walk melancholy, and devise

How they may cozen[129] merchants, fleece young heirs,

Creep into favor, by betraying men,

Rob churches, beg waste toys,[130] court city dames

Who shall undo their husbands for their sakes;

The baser rabble how to cheat and steal,

---

[123]Sixth-century B.C. philosopher and astronomer.

[124]Pupil of Anaximander.

[125]Fourth-century B.C. disciple of Plato.

[126]Alcmeon of Croton, pupil of Pythagoras, c. 500 B.C.; Nashe seems to think the names
indicate two people.

[127]Athenian philosopher, 400–325 B.C., founder of the Cynic sect, which is named after
kuwv, the dog, because of Diogenes' insistence on the need for shamelessness.

[128]Referring to the company of gods.

[129]cheat

[130]trifles

And yet be free from penalty of death:
So these word-warriors, lazy star-gazers,
Used to no labor but to louse themselves,
Had their heads filled with cozening fantasies.
They plotted how to make their poverty
Better esteemed of than high sovereignty,
They thought how they might plant a heaven on earth,
Whereof they would be principal low gods;
That heaven they called contemplation—
As much to say as a most pleasant sloth,
Which better I cannot compare than this,
That if a fellow, licensèd to beg,
Should all his lifetime go from fair to fair,
And buy gape-seed,[131] having no business else,
That contemplation, like an agèd weed,
Engendered thousand sects, and all those sects
Were but as these times, cunning shrouded rogues.
Grammarians some, and wherein differ they
From beggars that profess the pedlar's French?[132]
The poets next, slovenly tattered slaves,
That wander and sell ballads in the streets.
Historiographers others there be,
And they, like lazars[133] by the highway side,
That for a penny or a halfpenny,
Will call each knave a good faced gentleman,
Give honor unto tinkers for good ale,
Prefer a cobbler 'fore the black prince far,
If he bestow but blacking of their shoes:
And as it is the spittle-house's[134] guise
Over their gate to write the founder's names
Or on the outside of their walls at least,
In hope by their examples others moved
Will be more bountiful and liberal;

131Go sight-seeing
132Cant language of vagabonds.
133lepers
134Referring to a hospital or charitable institution.

So in the forefront of their chronicles,
Or *peroratione operis*,[135]
They learning's benefactors reckon up;
Who built this college, who gave that free school,
What king or queen advancèd scholars most,
And in their times what writers flourishèd.
Rich men and magistrates, whilst yet they live,
They flatter palpably, in hope of gain.
Smooth-tonguèd orators, the fourth in place,
Lawyers our commonwealth entitles them,
Mere swashbucklers and ruffianly mates,
That will for twelvepence make a doughty fray,
Set men for straws together by the ears.
Sky-measuring mathematicians,
Gold-breathing alchemists also we have,
Both which are subtle-witted humorists,
That get their meals by telling miracles,
Which they have seen in traveling the skies.
Vain boasters, liars, makeshifts, they are all;
Men that, removèd from their inkhorn terms,[136]
Bring forth no action worthy of their bread.
What should I speak of pale physicians,
Who as Fismenus *non nasutus*[137] was,
Upon a wager that his friends had laid,
Hired to live in a privy a whole year,
So are they hired for lucre and for gain,
All their whole life to smell on excrements.
[*WILL S:* Very true, for I have heard it for a proverb many a time and
oft, *hunc os fetidum*;[138] fah! he stinks like a physician.]
WINTER: Innumerable monstrous practices
Hath loitering contemplation brought forth more,
Which't were too long particular to recite:
Suffice they all conduce unto this end,

- -

[135]L.: peroration of the work.
[136]Pedantic expressions.
[137]Noseless Fismenus, a fictitious character.
[138]L.: he has a stinking mouth (said of the devil).

To banish labor, nourish slothfulness,
Pamper up lust, devise newfangled sins,
Nay, I will justify, there is no vice
Which learning and vile knowledge brought not in,
Or in whose praise some learnèd have not wrote.
The art of murder Machiavel hath penned;
Whoredom hath Ovid to uphold her throne,
And Aretine[139] of late in Italy,
Whose *Cortigiana* touched bawds their trade.
Gluttony Epicurus[140] doth defend,
And books of the art of cookery confirm,
Of which Platina[141] hath not writ the least.
Drunkenness of his good behavior
Hath testimonial from where he was born;
That pleasant work *de arte bibendi*,[142]
A drunken Dutchman spewed out few years since.
Nor wanteth sloth (although sloth's plague be want)
His paper pillars for to lean upon.
The praise of nothing pleads his worthiness.
Folly Erasmus sets a flourish on:
For baldness, a bald ass I have forgot,
Patched up a pamphletary periwig.
Slovenry Grobianus[143] magnifieth:
Sodomitry a cardinal commends,
And Aristotle necessary deems.
In brief, all books, divinity except,
Are nought but tables[144] of the devil's laws,
Poison wrapped up in sugared words,
Man's pride, damnation's props, the world's abuse.
Then censure, good my lord, what bookmen are:

---

[139]Pietro Aretino, 1492–1556, author of a number of works (some bawdy), including a play
La Cortigiana (*The Courtesan*), which Nashe seems to be confusing with something else.
[140]Athenian philosopher, 342/1-271/0 B.C., who did not advocate the excesses attributed to
him.
[141]Bartholomaeus Sacchi, fifteenth-century Italian writer.
[142]L.: *The Art of Drinking*, by one V. Obsopaeus, 1536.
[143]An imaginary German boor and patron of boors.
[144]Q "tales."

If they be pestilent members in a state;
He is unfit to sit at stern of state
That favors such as will o'erthrow his state.
Blest is that government where no art thrives;
Vox populi, vox Dei,
The vulgar's voice it is the voice of God.

'Tis Pity She's a Whore

John Ford
1627

Scene: Italy

#2 Female—Dramatic
> Annabella: a tragic young woman, 20s

> Annabella has allowed herself to be seduced by her brother, Giovanni. Here, she bemoans her sin as she wanders unhappily through the castle.

ANNABELLA: Pleasures, farewell, and all ye thriftless minutes
Wherein false joys have spun a weary life!
To these my fortunes now I take my leave.
Thou, precious Time, that swiftly rid'st in post
Over the world, to finish up the race
Of my last fate, here stay thy restless course,
And bear to ages that are yet unborn
A wretched, woeful woman's tragedy.
My conscience now stands up against[145] my lust
With depositions[146] character'd in guilt,[147]
(*Enter FRIAR [below].*)
And tells me I am lost: not I confess
Beauty that clothes the outside of the face
Is cursed if it be not cloth'd with grace.
Here like a turtle[148] mew'd up in a cage,
Unmated, I converse with air and walls,
And descant on my vile unhappiness.
O Giovanni, that hast had the spoil
Of thine own virtues and my modest fame,
Would thou hadst been less subject to those stars
That luckless reign'd at my nativity:
O would the scourge due to my black offense
Might pass from thee, that I alone might feel

---

[145]As a witness against.
[146]This seems to fit the legal metaphor better than the reading of Q.
[147]Apparently a punning phrase: (1) with gilt lettering; (2) written so as to expose Annabella's guilt.
[148]turtle-dove

The torment of an uncontrolled flame!
[*FRIAR:* (*Aside.*) What's this I hear?]
ANNABELLA: That man, that blessed friar,
Who join'd in ceremonial knot my hand
To him whose wife I now am, told me oft
I trod the path to death, and showed me how.
But they who sleep in lethargies of lust
Hug their confusion, making heaven unjust,
And so did I.
[*FRIAR:* (*Aside.*) Here's music to the soul!]
ANNABELLA: Forgive me, my good genius, and this once
Be helpful to my ends; let some good man
Pass this way, to whose trust I may commit
This paper double-lin'd with tears and blood:
Which being granted, here I sadly[149] vow
Repentance, and a leaving of that life
I long have died in.

149seriously

Titus Andronicus

William Shakespeare

1609

Scene: Rome

Female—Dramatic

Tamora: captive Queen of the Goths, now married to the Roman Emperor, 40s

When Titus Andronicus sacrifices one of her sons to appease the spirits of the members of his family slain in the war with the Goths, Tamora vows revenge. During a royal hunt, Tamora slips away with Aaron, her beloved Moorish attendant to plot her redress. When the two are discovered by Lavinia and her husband, Bassanius, the former accuses Tamora of adultery against the emperor with Aaron. Calling for her two remaining sons, Tamora tells the following lie, that she hopes will clear her of any adulterous charge while inciting the boys to murder Bassinius.

TAMORA: Have I not reason, think you, to look pale?
These two have 'ticed me hither to this place:
A barren detested vale, you see it is;
The trees, though summer, yet forlorn and lean,
O'ercome with moss and baleful mistletoe:
Here never shines the sun; here nothing breeds,
Unless the nightly owl or fatal raven:
And when they show'd me this abhorred pit,
They told me, here, at dead time of the night,
A thousand fiends, a thousand hissing snakes,
Ten thousand swelling toads, as many urchins,
Would make such fearful and confused cries
As any mortal body hearing it
Should straight fall mad, or else die suddenly.
No sooner had they told this hellish tale,
But straight they told me they would bind me here
Unto the body of a dismal yew,
And leave me to this miserable death:
And then they call'd me foul adultress,
Lascivious Goth, and all the bitterest terms
That ever ear did hear to such effect:
And, had you not by wondrous fortune come,

This vengeance on me had they executed.
Revenge it, as you love your mother's life,
Or be ye not henceforth call'd my children.

The Two Gentlemen of Verona
William Shakespeare
1592

Scene: Milan

Female—Serio-Comic
    Julia: a young woman in love, 16–20

> Julia has received a love letter from Proteus and, in a fit of pique, tears it up before
> having read it. Here, the impetuous young woman gathers all the scraps and tries to
> piece the letter back together again.

JULIA: O hateful hands, to tear such loving words!
Injurious wasps, to feed on such sweet honey
And kill the bees that yield it with your stings!
I'll kiss each several paper for amends.
Look, here is writ "kind Julia." Unkind Julia!
As in revenge of thy ingratitude,
I throw thy name against the bruising stones,
Trampling contemptuously on thy disdain.
And here is writ "love-wounded Proteus."
Poor wounded name! my bosom as a bed
Shall lodge thee till thy wound be thoroughly heal'd;
And thus I search it with a sovereign kiss.
But twice or thrice was "Proteus" written down.
Be calm, good wind, blow not a word away
Till I have found each letter in the letter,
Except mine own name: that some whirlwind bear
Unto a ragged fearful-hanging rock
And throw it thence into the raging sea!
Lo, here in one line is his name twice writ,
"Poor forlorn Proteus, passionate Proteus,
To the sweet Julia:" that I'll tear away.
And yet I will not, sith so prettily
He couples it to his complaining names.
Thus will I fold them one upon another:
Now kiss, embrace, contend, do what you will.

The Two Noble Kinsmen

John Fletcher and William Shakespeare
1634

Scene: Athens

#1 Female—Dramatic
Daughter: the daughter of the palace jailer, 18–20

The jailer's daughter has fallen in love with Palamon, a captive Thebian knight, and here agonizes over whether or not to help him escape from her father's prison.

DAUGHTER: Why should I love this gentleman? 'Tis odds
He never will affect[150] me: I am base,[151]
My father the mean keeper of his prison,
And he a prince. To marry him is hopeless,
To be his whore is witless. Out upon't,
What pushes[152] are we wenches driven to
When fifteen[153] once has found us! First I saw him;
I, seeing, thought he was a goodly man;
He has as much to please a woman in him—
If he please to bestow it so—as ever
These eyes yet look'd on; next, I pitied him,
And so would any young wench, o' my conscience,
That ever dream'd, or vow'd her maidenhead
To a young handsome man; then I lov'd him,
Extremely lov'd him, infinitely lov'd him;
And yet he had a cousin, fair as he too;
But in my heart was Palamon and there,
Lord, what a coil he keeps![154] To hear him
Sing in an evening, what a heaven it is!
And yet his songs are sad ones. Fairer spoken
Was never gentleman: when I come in
To bring him water in a morning, first
He bows his noble body, then salutes me, thus:

---

[150]love
[151]Of humble birth.
[152]efforts
[153]cf. V.i.130, V.ii.30.
[154]Turmoil he makes; Tilley, C 505.

"Fair, gentle maid, good morrow; may thy goodness
Get thee a happy husband." Once he kiss'd me:
I lov'd my lips the better ten days after;
Would he would do so ev'ry day! He grieves much,
And me as much to see his misery.
What should I do to make him know I love him?
For I would fain[155] enjoy him. Say I ventur'd
To set him free? What says the law then? Thus much
For law or kindred! I will do it,
And this night or tomorrow he shall love me.

#2 Female—Dramatic
    Daughter

> After defying both her father and her king, the jailer's daughter here plans to
> rendezvous with the escaped Palamon in the woods.

DAUGHTER: Let all the dukes and all the devils roar,
He is at liberty. I have ventur'd for him,
And out I have brought him. To a little wood
A mile hence I have sent him, where a cedar,
Higher than all the rest, spreads like a plane,
Fast by a brook; and there he shall keep close
Till I provide him files and food, for yet
His iron bracelets are not off. O love,
What a stout-hearted child thou art! My father
Durst better have endur'd cold iron[156] than done it.
I love him beyond love and beyond reason,
Or wit,[157] or safety. I have made him know it:
I care not, I am desperate; if the law
Find me and then condemn me for't, some wenches,
Some honest-hearted maids, will sing my dirge
And tell to memory my death was noble,
Dying almost a martyr. That way he takes,
I purpose is my way too. Sure, he cannot
Be so unmanly as to leave me here?

....

[155]gladly
[156]manacles
[157]sense

If he do, maids will not so easily
Trust men again. And yet he has not thank'd me
For what I have done; no, not so much as kiss'd me;
And that, methinks, is not so well: nor scarcely
Could I persuade him to become a freeman,
He made such scruples of the wrong he did
To me and to my father. Yet I hope,
When he considers more, this love of mine
Will take more root within him. Let him do
What he will with me, so he use me kindly,[158]
For use me so he shall or I'll proclaim him,
And to his face, no man. I'll presently
Provide him necessaries and pack my clothes up,
And where there is a path of[159] ground I'll venture,
So he be with me; by him, like a shadow,
I'll ever dwell. Within this hour the hubbub
Will be all o'er the prison: I am then
Kissing the man they look for! Farewell, father;
Get[160] many more such prisoners, and such daughters,
And shortly you may keep yourself.[161] Now to him!

#5 Female—Dramatic
    Emilia: sister-in-law of Theseus, 20s

    Palamon and Arcite, two knights of Thebes, have both fallen in love with Emilia,
    who here agonizes over which of the two she loves in return.

EMILIA: Yet I may bind those wounds up, that must open
And bleed to death for my sake else: I'll choose
And end their strife. Two such young handsome men
Shall never fall for me; their weeping mothers,
Shall never curse my cruelty. Good heaven,
What a sweet face has Arcite! If wise nature,
With all her best endowments, all those beauties
She sows into the births of noble bodies,

---

[158](1) benevolently; (2) sexually, according to nature.
[159]on
[160](1) obtain; (2) beget.
[161](1) be a prisoner in your own jail; (2) live alone.

Were here a mortal woman and had in her
The coy denials of young maids, yet doubtless
She would run mad for this man. What an eye,
Of what a fiery sparkle and quick[162] sweetness,
Has this young prince! Here love himself sits smiling!
Just such another wanton Ganymede[163]
Set Jove afire with and enforc'd the god
Snatch up the goodly boy and set him by him,
A shining constellation. What a brow,
Of what a spacious majesty, he carries,
Arch'd like the great-eyed Juno's, but far sweeter,
Smoother than Pelops' shoulder![164] Fame and honor,
Methinks, from hence, as from a promontory
Pointed[165] in heaven, should clap their wings and sing
To all the under world the loves and fights
Of gods, and such men near[166] 'em. Palamon
Is but his foil;[167] to him, a mere dull shadow;
He's swarth[168] and meager,[169] of an eye as heavy
As if he had lost his mother; a still temper,
No stirring in him, no alacrity,
Of all this[170] sprightly sharpness, not a smile.
Yet these that we count errors may become[171] him:
Narcissus[172] was a sad boy but a heavenly.
O, who can find the bent of woman's fancy?
I am a fool, my reason is lost in me,
I have no choice and I have lied so lewdly[173]
That women ought to beat me. On my knees
I ask thy pardon. Palamon, thou art alone

....

[162]lively
[163]Ovid *Metamorphoses* x. 155–161.
[164]The left shoulder of Pelops was made of ivory; Ovid *Metamorphoses* vi. 403–411.
[165]Coming to a point.
[166]I.e., in achievement.
[167]Dull metal used behind or around a jewel to set off its brilliance by contrast.
[168]of dark complexion
[169]thin
[170]I.e., Arcite's.
[171]suit
[172]cf. II.ii.119–121.
[173]ignorantly

And only beautiful, and these the eyes,
These the bright lamps of beauty, that command
And threaten love; and what young maid dare cross 'em?
What a bold gravity, and yet inviting,
Has this brown manly face! O love, this only
From this hour is complexion.[174] Lie there, Arcite:
Thou art a changeling[175] to him, a mere gipsy,[176]
And this the noble body. I am sotted,
Utterly lost; my virgin's faith[177] has fled me;
For if my brother, but even now, had ask'd me
Whether[178] I lov'd, I had run mad for Arcite;
Now if my sister, more for Palamon.
Stand both together. Now, come ask me, brother;
Alas, I know not. Ask me now, sweet sister;
I may go look.[179] What a mere child is fancy,
That having two fair gauds[180] of equal sweetness,
Cannot distinguish, but must cry for both!

---

[174]The only handsome color; current taste was for fair skin.
[175]A child secretly substituted for another in infancy, therefore usually ugly.
[176]The normal sense, "dark-skinned," seems oddly inappropriate to Arcite, whose skin has been described as lighter than Palamon's.
[177]Dedication to virginity.
[178]Which of them.
[179]I am at a loss.
[180]toys

The Winter's Tale

William Shakespeare
1611

Scene: Sicilia

#1 Female—Dramatic
Hermione: a queen wrongly accused of adultery, 20–30

Leonates has accused his wife of bearing the child of his one-time friend, Polixenes. When she is formally charged with high treason, Hermione makes the following speech in her own defense.

HERMIONE: Since what I am to say must be but that
Which contradicts my accusation and
The testimony on my part no other
But what comes from myself, it shall scarce boot me
To say "not guilty": mine integrity
Being counted falsehood, shall, as I express it,
Be so received. But thus: if powers divine
Behold our human actions, as they do,
I doubt not then but innocence shall make
False accusation blush and tyranny
Tremble at patience. You, my lord, best know,
Who least will seem to do so, my past life
Hath been as continent, as chaste, as true,
As I am now unhappy; which is more
Than history can pattern, though devised
And play'd to take spectators. For behold me
A fellow of the royal bed, which owe
A moiety of the throne, a great king's daughter,
The mother to a hopeful prince, here standing
To prate and talk for life and honour 'fore
Who please to come and hear. For life, I prize it
As I weigh grief, which I would spare: for honour,
'Tis a derivative from me to mine,
And only that I stand for. I appeal
To your own conscience, sir, before Polixenes
Came to your court, how I was in your grace,

How merited to be so; since he came,
With what encounter so uncurrent I
Have strain'd to appear thus: if one jot beyond
The bound of honour, or in act or will
That way inclining, harden'd be the hearts
Of all that hear me, and my near'st of kin
Cry fie upon my grave!

#2 Female—Dramatic
     Hermione

     Here, the accused queen demands that she be judged by the Delphic Oracle.

HERMIONE: Sir, spare your threats:
The bug which you would fright me with I seek.
To me can life be no commodity:
The crown and comfort of my life, your favour,
I do give lost; for I do feel it gone,
But know not how it went. My second joy
And first-fruits of my body, from his presence
I am bar'd, like one infectious. My third comfort,
Starr'd most unluckily, is from my breast,
The innocent milk in it most innocent mouth,
Haled out to murder: myself on every post
Proclaim'd a strumpet: with immodest hatred
The child-bed privilege denied, which 'longs
To women of all fashion; lastly, hurried
Here to this place, i' the open air, before
I have got strength of limit. Now, my liege,
Tell me what blessings I have here alive,
That I should fear to die? Therefore proceed.
But yet hear this; mistake me not; no life,
I prize it not a straw, but for mine honour,
Which I would free, if I shall be condemn'd
Upon surmises, all proofs sleeping else
But what your jealousies awake, I tell you
'Tis rigour and now law. Your honours all,
I do refer me to the oracle:
Apollo be my judge!

The Witch

Thomas Middleton

1619–27

Scene: Ravenna

Female—Dramatic

Francisca: a young woman struggling to cope with illegitimate pregnancy, 20s

Francisca is nearing the time when she will no longer be able to keep her pregnancy a secret from her family. Here, she ponders her unfortunate circumstances.

FRANCISCA: I have the hardest fortune, I think, of a hundred
   gentlewomen.
Some can make merry with a friend seven year
And nothing seen; as perfect a maid still,
To the world's knowledge, as she came from rocking.
But 'twas my luck, at the first hour, forsooth,
To prove too fruitful. Sure, I'm near my time.
I'm yet but a young scholar, I may fail
In my account; but certainly I do not.
These bastards come upon poor venturing gentlewomen ten to one
faster than your legitimate children. If I had been married, I'll be
hanged if I had been with child so soon now. When they are once
husbands they'll be whipped ere they take such pains as a friend will
do: come by water to the back-door at midnight; there stay perhaps
an hour in all weathers with a pair of reeking watermen laden with
bottles of wine, chewets and currant-custards. I may curse those egg-
pies; they are meat that help forward too fast.
This hath been usual with me night by night,
Honesty forgive me, when my brother has been
Dreaming of no such junkets; yet he hath fared
The better for my sake, though he little think
For what, nor must he ever. My friend promised me
To provide safely for me, and devise
A means to save my credit here i'th'house.
My brother sure would kill me if he knew't,
And powder-up my friend and all his kindred
For an East Indian voyage.

The Witch of Edmonton

William Rowley, Thomas Dekker, and John Ford
1628

Scene: Edmonton

#1 Female—Dramatic
Elizabeth Sawyer: a hag, 50–70

Believed by all to be a witch, Elizabeth here reveals her desire to live up to everyone's expectations so that she may wreak revenge on those who have abused her.

ELIZABETH SAWYER: Still vexed! Still tortured! That curmudgeon
Banks
Is ground of all my scandal. I am shunned
And hated like a sickness, made a scorn
To all degrees and sexes. I have heard old beldams
Talk of familiars in the shape of mice,
Rats, ferrets, weasels and I wot not what,
That have appeared and sucked, some say, their blood.
But by what means they came acquainted with them
I'm now ignorant. Would some power, good or bad,
Instruct me which way I might be revenged
Upon this churl, I'd go out of myself
And give this fury leave to dwell within
This ruined cottage ready to fall with age,
Abjure all goodness, be at hate with prayer,
And study curses, imprecations,
Blasphemous speeches, oaths, detested oaths,
Or anything that's ill; so I might work
Revenge upon this miser, this black cur
That barks and bites, and sucks the very blood
Of me and of my credit. 'Tis all one
To be a witch as to be counted one.
Vengeance, shame, ruin light upon that canker!

Elizabeth has been sent a dog-like familiar from the dark lord she has promised to serve. The familiar has committed much mischief at her bequest and has become very dear to the old witch. Here, she calls for her satanic familiar.

ELIZABETH SAWYER: Still wronged by every slave, and not a dog
Bark in his dame's defence? I am called witch,
Yet am myself bewitched from doing harm.
Have I given up myself to thy black lust
Thus to be scorned? Not see me in three days!
I'm lost without my Tomalin. Prithee come.
Revenge to me is sweeter far than life;
Thou art my raven on whose coal-black wings
Revenge comes flying to me. O my best love!
I am on fire, even in the midst of ice,
Raking my blood up till my shrunk knees feel
Thy curled head leaning on them. Come then, my darling.
If in the air thou hover'st, fall upon me
In some dark cloud; and as I oft have seen
Dragons and serpents in the elements,
Appear thou now so to me. Art thou i'th' sea?
Muster up all the monsters from the deep,
And be the ugliest of them. So that my bulch
Show but his swart cheek to me, let earth cleave
And break from hell, I care not! Could I run
Like a swift powder-mine beneath the world,
Up would I blow it all to find out thee,
Though I lay ruined in it. Not yet come!
I must then fall to my old prayer,
Sanctibiceter nomen tuum.

A Woman Killed with Kindness

Thomas Heywood
1603

Scene: England

Female—Dramatic
> Anne: a woman guilty of infidelity, 30s

> Anne has been lured into an unfortunate dalliance by the unscrupulous Wendoll, a supposed friend of her husband's. When the affair is found out, she tearfully abases herself in front of her husband.

ANNE: I would I had no tongue, no ears, no eyes,
No apprehension, no capacity.[181]
When do you spurn me like a dog? When tread me
Under your feet? When drag me by the hair?
Though I deserve a thousand thousand fold
More than you can inflict, yet, once my husband,
For womanhood—to which I am a shame
Though once an ornament—even for His sake
That hath redeem'd our souls, mark not my face
Nor hack me with your sword, but let me go
Perfect and undeformed to my tomb!
I am not worthy that I should prevail
In the least suit, not to speak to you,
No look on you, nor to be in your presence;
Yet as an abject[182] this one suit I crave,
This granted I am ready for my grave.

---

[181]That is, no powers of reason.
[182]outcast

Women Beware Women

Thomas Middleton
1657

Scene: Florence

Female—Dramatic
>   Livia: a concerned sister, 30–40

>   When Livia discovers that her brother, Hippolito, has fallen in love with their niece,
>   Isabella, she does her best to provide him with sympathetic advice.

LIVIA: Is the world
So populous in women, and creation
So prodigal in beauty and so various,
Yet does love turn thy point[183] to thine own blood?
'Tis somewhat too unkindly;[184] must thy eye
Dwell evilly on the fairness of thy kinred,
And seek not where it should? it is confin'd
Now in a narrower prison than was made for't:
It is allow'd a stranger, and where bounty
Is made the great man's honour, 'tis ill husbandry
To spare, and servants shall have small thanks for't.
So he heaven's bounty seems to scorn and mock,
That spares free means, and spends of his own stock.
[*HIPPOLITO:* Never was man's misery so soon summ'd[185] up,
Counting how truly.]
LIVIA: Nay, I love you so,
That I shall venture much to keep a change[186] from you
So fearful as this grief will bring upon you.
'Faith it even kills me, when I see you faint
Under a reprehension, and I'll leave it,
Though I know nothing can be better for you:
Prethee (sweet Brother) let not passion waste
The goodness of thy time, and of thy fortune:

---

[183]With a sexual quibble.
[184]With a quibble on "kind" in the sense of "kin."
[185]The quarto has "sow'd," almost certainly a misprint for "som'd."
[186]I.e., in her.

Thou keep'st the treasure of that life I love
As dearly as mine own; and if you think
My former words too bitter, which were minist'red
By truth and zeal, 'tis but a hazarding
Of grace and virtue, and I can bring forth
As pleasant fruits as sensuality wishes
In all her teeming longings; this I can do.
[*HIPPOLITO:* Oh nothing that can make my wishes perfect!]
LIVIA: I would that love of yours were pawn'd to't, Brother,
And as soon lost that way as I could win.
Sir, I could give as shrewd a lift to chastity[187]
As any she that wears a tongue in Florence.
Sh'ad need be a good horse-woman, and sit fast,
Whom my strong argument could not fling at last.
Prethee take courage, man; though I should counsel
Another to despair, yet I am pitiful
To thy afflictions, and will venture hard;
I will not name for what, 'tis not handsome;
Find you the proof,[188] and praise me.
[*HIPPOLITO:* Then I fear me
I shall not praise you in haste.]
LIVIA: This is the comfort,
You are not the first (Brother) has attempted
Things more forbidden than this seems to be:
I'll minister all cordials now to you,
Because I'll cheer you up sir.

---

[187]as cunningly trap the chaste
[188]when you find the proof

The Wonder of Women or The Tragedy of Sophonisba

John Marston

1606

Scene: Libya

#2 Female—Dramatic
   Sophonisba: Princess of Carthage and wife of Massinissa, 20s

   Sophonisba rejected the suit of Syphax of Libya in favor of Massinissa. When an
   enraged Syphax joins forces with the Roman army in a brutal attack on Carthage,
   Massinissa is forced to abandon their bridal bed to help defend the city. As the battle
   rages, Sophonisba reflects on their fate.

SOPHONISBA: My lords, 'tis most unusual such sad haps
Of sudden horror should intrude 'mong beds
Of soft and private loves; but strange events
Excuse strange forms. O you that know our blood,
Revenge if I do feign. I here protest,
Though my lord leave his wife a very maid,
Even this night, instead of my soft arms
Clasping his well-strung limbs with glossful steel,
What's safe to Carthage shall be sweet to me.
I must not, nor am I once ignorant
My choice of love hath given this sudden danger
To yet strong Carthage. 'Twas I lost the fight;
My choice vexed Syphax; enraged Syphax struck
Arms' fate; yet Sophonisba not repents:
O we were gods if that we knew events.
But let my lord leave Carthage, quit his virtue,
I will not love him; yet must honour him,
As still good subjects must bad princes. Lords,
From the most ill-graced hymeneal bed
That ever Juno frowned at, I entreat
That you'll collect from our loose-formed speech
This firm resolve: that no low appetite
Of my sex' weakness can or shall o'ercome
Due grateful service unto you or virtue.

Witness, ye gods, I never until now
Repined at my creation. Now I wish
I were no woman, that my arms might speak
My heart to Carthage. But in vain: my tongue
Swears I am woman still. I talk too long.

#3 Female—Dramatic
Erictho: a witch, any age

Syphax's unrequited passion for Sophonisba brings him close to madness. In desperation, he summons the enchantress, Erictho, who promises him that the princess will soon share his bed.

ERICTHO: Here, Syphax, here. Quake not, for know
I know thy thoughts. Thou wouldst entreat our power
Nice Sophonisba's passion to enforce
To thy affection. Be all full of Jove,
'Tis done, 'tis done. To us heaven, earth, sea, air,
And Fate itself obeys. The beasts of death
And all terrors angry gods invented,
T'afflict th'ignorance of patient man,
Tremble at us. The rolled-up snake uncurls
His twisted knots at our affrighting voice.
Are we incensed? The king of flames grows pale,
Lest he be choked with black and earthy fumes,
Which our charms raise. Be joyed, make proud thy lust.
I do not pray, you gods: my breath's "You must."
[SYPHAX: Deep-knowing spirit, mother of all high
Mysterious science, what may Syphax yield
Worthy thy art, by which my soul's thus eased?
The gods first made me live, but thou live pleased.]
ERICTHO: Know then, our love, hard by the reverend ruins
Of a once glorious temple reared to Jove,
Whose very rubbish, like the pitied fall
Of virtue most unfortunate, yet bears
A deathless majesty, though now quite razed,
Hurled down by wrath and lust of impious kings,
So that, where holy Flamens wont to sing
Sweet hymns to heaven, there the daw and crow,

The ill-voiced raven and still-cattering pie
Send out ungrateful sound and loathsome filth;
Where statues and Jove's acts were vively limned,
Boys with black coals draw the veiled parts of nature
And lecherous actions of imagined lust;
Where tombs and beauteous urns of well-dead men
Stood in assurèd rest, the shepherd now
Unloads his belly; corruption most abhorred
Mingling itself with their renownèd ashes.
Ourself quakes at it.
There once a charnel-house, now a vast cave,
Over whose brow a pale and untrod grove
Throws out her heavy shade; the mouth, thick arms
Of darksome yew, sun-proof, for ever choke.
Within rests barren darkness; fruitless drought
Pines in eternal night. The steam of hell
Yields not so lazy air. There, that's my cell;
From thence a charm, which Jove dare not hear twice,
Shall force her to thy bed. But, Syphax, know,
Love is the highest rebel to our art.
Therefore I charge thee, by the fear of all
Which thou knowest dreadful, or more, by ourself,
As with swift haste she passeth to thy bed,
And easy to thy wishes yields, speak not one word,
Nor dare, as thou dost fear thy loss of joys,
T'admit one light, one light.

A Chaste Maid in Cheapside

Thomas Middleton
1613

Scene: England

Male—Serio-Comic
> Allwit: a man whose wife is having an affair, 20–30

> Allwit's wife is carrying Sir Walter's child. The knight has arranged to keep the Allwits in fine style as they await the birth of the child. Here, broad-minded Allwit contentedly contemplates his good fortune.

ALLWIT: The founder's come to town; I am like a man
Finding a table furnished to his hand,
As mine is still to me, prays for the founder;
Bless the right worshipful, the good founder's life.
I thank him, h'as maintained my house this ten years,
Not only keeps my wife, but a[1] keeps me,
And all my family,[2] I am at his table,
He gets me all my children, and pays the nurse,
Monthly, or weekly, puts me to nothing,
Rent, nor church duties, not so much as the scavenger.[3]
The happiest state that ever man was born to.
I walk out in a morning, come to breakfast,
Find excellent cheer, a good fire in winter,
Look in my coal house about midsummer eve,
That's full, five or six chaldron,[4] new laid up;
Look in my back yard, I shall find a steeple
Made up with Kentish faggots,[5] which o'erlooks
The waterhouse and the windmills,[6] I say nothing
But smile, and pin the door. When she lies in,

....

[1]he
[2]Includes servants as well as children.
[3]Officer of the town who employed the poor to sweep the street; Stow says Bread St. ward, which contained part of Cheapside, had eight.
[4]A dry measure of 36 bushels of coal; the coal trade between Newcastle and London grew tenfold between 1545 and 1625 and while Shakespeare was in London the price per chaldron rose from four shillings to nine.
[5]Bundles of brushwood, about eight feet long and one foot through; much London firewood came from Kent.
[6]Built near Broken Wharf in 1594 by Bevis Bulmer "to convey Thames water into men's houses of West Cheap, about Paul's, Fleet Street, &c" (*Survey*, I, 8). *Visscher's View of London* (1616) shows the waterhouse with a windmill on the top.

As now she's even upon the point of grunting,
A lady lies not in like her; there's her embossings,
Embroiderings, spanglings, and I know not what,
As if she lay with all the gaudy shops
In Gresham's Burse[7] about her; then her restoratives,
Able to set up a young 'pothecary,
And richly stock the foreman of a drug shop;
Her sugar by whole loaves, her wines by rundlets.[8]
I see these things, but like a happy man,
I pay for none at all, yet fools think's[9] mine;
I have the name, and in his gold I shine.
And where some merchants would in soul kiss hell,
To buy a paradise for their wives, and dye
Their conscience in the bloods of prodigal heirs,[10]
To deck their night-piece,[11] yet all this being done,
Eaten with jealousy to the inmost bone—
As what affliction nature more constrains,
Than feed the wife plump for another's veins?—
These torments stand I freed of, I am as clear
From jealousy of a wife as from the charge.
O two miraculous blessings; 'tis the knight
Hath took that labour all out of my hands;
I may sit still and play; he's jealous for me—
Watches her steps, sets spies—I live at ease;
He has both the cost and torment; when the strings
Of his heart frets,[12] I feed, laugh, or sing,
La dildo, dildo la dildo, la dildo dildo de dildo.[13]

....

[7]The Royal Exchange, "whose founder was Sir Thomas Gresham Knight, agent to her
Majesty, built 1566–8 for the confluence and commerce of merchants" (John Speed, *The
Theatre of . . . Great Britain* (1611), fol. 852).

[8]Small barrels; large rundlets held between 12 and 18½ gallons, small between a pint and
four gallons.

[9]think it's

[10]"Wickedly extort money from spend-thrift sons of the gentry to buy clothing and
jewellery for their whores." Gulling "prodigal heirs" is a major theme in Middleton's
Michaelmas Term (c. 1606).

[11]mistress, bedfellow

[12]The heart was supposed to be braced with strings, which frayed and broke under
emotional stress; the fret of a musical instrument was a ring of gut, now wood or metal, on
the fingerboard to regulate fingering.

[13]Chorus with ironic overtones since a dildo is a substitute phallus.

A Fair Quarrel

Thomas Middleton and William Rowley
1617

Scene: England

Male—Dramatic
Captain Ager: a young soldier defending his family's honor, 20s

When Captain Ager is accused of being illegitimate, he challenges his accuser to a duel. Here, he rages against this unwholesome slight to his mother.

CAPTAIN AGER: The son of a whore?
There is not such another murdering piece
In all the stock of calumny; it kills
At one report two reputations,
A mother's and a son's.[14] If it were possible
That souls could fight after the bodies fell,
This were a quarrel for 'em. He should be one indeed
That never heard of heaven's joys or hell's torments
To fight this out; I am too full of conscience,
Knowledge and patience, to give justice to't;
So careful of my eternity,[15] which consists
Of upright actions, that unless I knew
It were a truth I stood for, any coward
Might make my breast his footpace.[16] And who lives
That can assure the truth of his conception,[17]
More than a mother's carriage makes it hopeful?
And is't not miserable valor then
That man should hazard all upon things doubtful?
Oh, there's the cruelty of my foe's advantage!
Could but my soul resolve my cause were just,

---

[14]One "deprived of naturall honor, is incapable of any other . . ."; a mother's unchastity deprives her children of native honor, without which perfect honor cannot be acquired (Sir John Kepers, *The Courtiers Academie*, 1598, sigs. P3r–P3v).

[15]As Sampson notes, p. 393, Ager's need to have reassurance of his mother's purity becomes a credible motive in the light of Elizabethan acceptance of the duel as a trial by combat. In this trial the man who defends a lie provokes the wrath of God (and consequently his own defeat) and may suffer death and damnation. A prudent man will not thus hazard all upon things doubtful.

[16]A carpet, a mat, or a step in a staircase.

[17]Be certain of his legitimacy.

Earth's mountain, nor sea's surge should hide him from me;
E'en to hell's threshold would I follow him
And see the slanderer in before I left him!
But as it is, it fears me; and I never
Appear'd too conscionably just till now.
My good opinion of her life and virtues
Bids me go on, and fain would I be rul'd by't;
But when my judgment tells me she's but woman,
Whose frailty let in death to all mankind,
My valor shrinks at that. Certain she's good;
There only wants but my assurance in't,
And all things then were perfect. How I thirst for't!
Here comes the only she that could resolve,
But 'tis too vild[18] a question to demand indeed.

---

[18]Equivalent to "vile" in its adjectival senses. *Vild* is a very common form in the early seventeenth century.

A Mad World, My Masters

Thomas Middleton
1606

Scene: London

Male—Serio-Comic
> Master Penitent Brothel: a young man up to no good, 20–30

> A man of questionable morality, Penitent here contemplates the possibility of committing adultery.

MASTER PENITENT BROTHEL: Ha! Read that place again. "Adultery[19]

Draws the divorce 'twixt heaven and the soul."
Accursed man, that stand'st divorc'd from heaven,
Thou wretched unthrift, that has play'd away
Thy eternal portion at a minute's game
To please the flesh, hast blotted out thy name,
Where were thy nobler meditations busied
That they durst trust this body with itself,
This natural drunkard that undoes us all
And makes our shame apparent in our fall?
Then let my blood pay for't, and vex and boil.
My soul, I know, would never grieve to th' death
The eternal spirit that feeds her with his breath.
Nay, I that knew the price of life and sin,
What crown is kept for continence, what for lust,
The end of man, and glory of that end
As endless as the giver,
To dote on weakness, slime, corruption, woman!
What is she, took asunder from her clothes?
Being ready, she consists of hundred pieces
Much like your German clock, and near allied;[20]
Both are so nice they cannot go for pride,
Beside a greater fault, but too well known,

[19]The speech of remorse is common in Middleton's plays; see *A Chaste Maid in Cheapside,* V.i.67 ff., *The Spanish Gypsy,* III.i.l ff.

[20]"An allusion to the cumbersome and complicated machinery of our first clocks, which came from Germany" (Dyce).

They'll strike to ten when they should stop at one.
Within these three days the next meeting's fix'd;
If I meet then, hell and my soul be mix'd.
My lodging I know constantly, she not knows.
Sin's hate is the best gift that sin bestows;
I'll ne'er embrace her more; never, bear witness, never.

A Woman Killed with Kindness

Thomas Heywood
1603

Scene: England

Male—Dramatic
> Wendoll: a man who has seduced his friend's wife, 30s

> The unscrupulous Wendoll has managed to lure the lovely Anne into an illicit affair. When Anne is subsequently banished by her husband, Wendoll realizes that he is responsible for her unhappy fate.

WENDOLL: Pursued with horror of a guilty soul
And with the sharp scourge of repentance lashed,
I fly from my own shadow. O my stars!
What have my parents in their lives deserved
That you should lay this penance on their son?
When I but think of Master Frankford's love
And lay it to my treason, or compare
My murd'ring him for his relieving me,
It strikes a terror like a lightning's flash
To scorch my blood up. Thus I, like the owl
Ashamed of day, live in these shadowy woods
Afraid of every leaf or murmuring blast,
Yet longing to receive some perfect[21] knowledge
How he hath dealt with her. (*Sees Anne.*) O my sad fate!
Here, and so far from home, and thus attended!
O god, I have divorced the truest turtles[22]
That ever lived together, and being divided
In several[23] places, make their several moan;
She in the fields laments and he at home.
So poets write that Orpheus made the trees
And stones to dance to his melodious harp,
Meaning the rustic and the barbarous hinds,[24]
That had no understanding part in them;

---

[21]correct
[22]turtle doves
[23]separate
[24]folk

So she from these rude carters tears extracts,
Making their flinty hearts with grief to rise
And draw down rivers from their rocky eyes.

All Fools

George Chapman
1605

Scene: Florence

#1 Male—Serio-Comic
      Gostanzo: a foolish old knight, 50–60

      Here, this talkative braggart lectures his son on the finer points of entertaining
      ladies.

GOSTANZO: Ah, errant[25] sheepshead, hast thou liv'd thus long,
And dar'st not look a woman in the face?
Though I desire especially to see
My son a husband, shall I therefore have him
Turn absolute cullion?[26] Let's see, kiss thy hand.
Thou kiss thy hand? Thou wip'st thy mouth, by th' mass.
Fie on thee, clown. They say the world's grown finer,
But I for my part never saw young men
Worse fashion'd and brought up than nowadays.
'Sfoot, when myself was young, was not I kept
As far from court as you? I think I was.
And yet my father on a time invited
The Duchess[27] of his house. I, being then
About some five-and-twenty years of age,
Was thought the only man to entertain her.
I had my congé—plant myself of one leg,
Draw back the tother with a deep-fetch'd honor,[28]
Then with a bel-regard[29] advant[30] mine eye
With boldness on her very visnomy.
Your dancers all were counterfeits to me.
And for discourse in my fair mistress' presence
I did not as you barren gallants do,

----

[25]absolute, unmitigated
[26]"A base, despicable, or vile fellow; a rascal" (*OED*).
[27]Family matriarch, head of his house.
[28]Curtsy or bow.
[29]flirtatious glance
[30]advance

Fill my discourses up drinking[31] tobacco,
But on the present furnish'd evermore
With tales and practic'd speeches—as sometimes,
"What is't o'clock?" "What stuff's this petticoat?"
"What cost the making?" "What the fringe and all?"
And what she had under her petticoat,
And such-like witty compliments. And for need,
I could have written as good prose and verse
As the most beggarly poet of 'em all,
Either acrostic, exordium,[32]
Epithalamions, satires, epigrams,
Sonnets in dozens,[33] or your quatorzains[34]
In any rhyme, masculine, feminine,
Or sdrucciola,[35] or couplets blank verse.
Y'are but bench-whistlers[36] nowadays to them
That were in our times. Well, about your husbandry.
Go, for i'faith, th'art fit for nothing else.

#2 Male—Serio-Comic
      Valerio: Gostanzo's son, 20s

    Here, Valerio offers a drunken salute to the age he lives in; where all are fools being
    fooled by other fools.

VALERIO: Is't come to this? Then will I make a speech in praise of this
reconcilement, including therein the praise and honor of the most fash-
ionable and authentical HORN. Stand close, gentles, and be silent. (*He
gets into a chair.*)
[*GOSTANZO:* Come on. Let's hear his wit in this potable[37] humor.]
VALERIO: The course of the world (like the life of man) is said to be
divided into several ages. As we into infancy, childhood, youth, and so

. . . .

[31]inhaling
[32]Not a literary form as such, but simply the rhetorical term for the beginning of something,
particularly an oration or discourse.
[33]"Probably songs or sonnets of twelve lines in length" (Parrott).
[34]French term for sonnet.
[35]A rhyme word in which the third syllable from the end of the word is accented, i.e., a
dactylic rime. So called from the italian *sdrucciolo* (*slippery*).
[36]do-nothings
[37]The *OED* cites this as the only example of the rare use of the term meaning "appropriate
to drinking." More probably it means drunken.

forward to old age, so the world into the golden age, the silver, the brass, the iron, the leaden, the wooden, and now into this present age, which we term the horned age. Not that but former ages have enjoyed this benefit as well as our times, but that in ours it is more common, and nevertheless precious. It is said that in the golden age of the world the use of gold was not then known: an argument of the simplicity of that age. Lest therefore succeeding ages should hereafter impute the same fault to us which we lay upon the first age, that we, living in the horned age of the world, should not understand the use, the virtue, the honor, and the very royalty of the horn, I will in brief sound the praises thereof that they who are already in possession of it may bear their heads aloft as being proud of such lofty accouterments, and they that are but in possibility may be ravished with a desire to be in possession.

A trophy so honorable and unmatchably powerful that it is able to raise any man from a beggar to an emperor's fellow, a duke's fellow, a nobleman's fellow, alderman's fellow; so glorious that it deserves to be worn (by most opinions) in the most conspicuous place about a man. For what worthier crest can you bear than the horn, which if it might be seen with our mortal eyes, what a wonderful spectacle would there be, and how highly they would ravish the beholders? But their substance is incorporal, not falling under sense, nor mixed of the gross concretion of elements, but a quintessence beyond them, a spiritual essence, invisible and everlasting.

And this hath been the cause that many men have called their being in question, whether there be such a thing in *rerum natura*,[38] or not, because they are not to be seen; as though nothing were that were not to be seen! Who ever saw the wind? Yet what wonderful effects are seen of it! It drives the clouds, yet no man sees it. It rocks the house, bears down trees, castles, steeples, yet who sees it? In like sort does your horn. It swells the forehead, yet none sees it. It rocks the cradle, yet none sees it. So that you plainly perceive sense is no judge of essence. The moon to any man's sense seems to be horned, yet who knows not the moon to be ever perfectly round? So likewise your heads seem ever to be round, when indeed they are oftentimes horned. For their original, it is unsearchable. Natural they are not, for where[39] is

---

[38]In the nature of things.

beast born with horns, more than with teeth? Created they were not, for *ex nihilo nihil fil.*[40] Then will you ask me, how came they into the world? I know not, but I am sure women brought them into this part of the world, howsoever some doctors are of opinion that they came in with the Devil. And not unlike, for as the Devil brought sin into the world, but the woman brought it to the man, so it may very well be that the Devil brought horns into the world, but the woman brought them to the man.

For their power, it is general over the world. No nation so barbarious, no country so proud, but doth equal homage to the horn. Europa, when she was carried through the sea by the Saturnian bull,[41] was sad (for fear of falling) to have held by the horn, and what is this but a plain showing to us, that all Europe, which took name from that Europa,[42] should likewise hold by the horn. So that I say it is universal over the face of the world, general over the face of Europe, and common over the face of this country. What city, what town, what village, what street, nay, what house, can quit itself of this prerogative? I have read that the lion once made a proclamation[43] through all the forest, that all horned beasts should depart forthwith upon pain of death. If this proclamation should be made through our forest, Lord, what pressing, what running, what flying would there be even from all the parts of it! He that had but a bunch of flesh in his head would away, and some, foolishly fearful, would imagine the shadow of his ears to be horns. Alas, how desert would this forest be left!

To conclude: for their force it is irrevitable,[44] for were they not irrevitable, then might either properness of person secure a man, or wisdom prevent 'em, or greatness exempt, or riches redeem them. But

....

[39]*Collier;* there *Q.*

[40]Nothing is made from nothing.

[41]Zeus, son of Saturn, who disguised as a bull, kidnapped Europa and carried her off to Crete.

[42]*Collier;* Europa *Q.*

[43]A common joke in the Renaissance, apparently not one of Aesop's fables, though St. Thomas More identifies it as such. For the entire fable, see More's *History of Richard III,* ed. R. S. Sylvester (The Yale Edition of More's *Complete Works*), III, 93, 269.

[44]The *OED* cites this example for its only use in English of the word *irrenitble* ("not to be struggled against"), deriving it from *ir* plus the Latin *reniti,* meaning to struggle against, resist. But it is more probably a portmanteau word incorporating inevitable and irrevocable and meaning something in between both. It does not seem to be a misprint since it occurs with the same spelling two times very close together in two separate lines.

present experience hath taught us that in this case all these stand in no stead. For we see the properest men take part of them, the best wits cannot avoid them (for then should poets be no cuckholds). Nor can money redeem them, for then would rich men fine for[45] their horns, as they do for offices. But this is held for a maxim, that there are more rich cuckolds than poor. Lastly, for continuance of the horn, it is undeterminable[46] till death. Neither do they determine with the wife's death (howsoever ignorant writers hold opinion they do). For as when a knight dies, his lady still retains the title of lady; when a company is cast,[47] yet the captain still retains the title of captain; so though the wife die, by whom this title came to her husband, yet by the courtesy of the City, he shall be a cuckold during life, let all ignorant asses prate what they list.

---

[45]pay money to escape
[46]without ending
[47]dismissed

Arden of Feversham

Anonymous
1592

Scene: England

#1 Male—Serio-Comic
 Michael: a hapless young servant, 16–20

Master Arden's young wife and her lover have hatched a plot to murder him. When Michael discovers their plan, he agonizes whether or not he should take action.

MICHAEL: Conflicting thoughts, encampèd in my breast,
Awake me with the echo of their strokes,
And I, a judge to censure either side,
Can give to neither wishèd victory.
My master's kindness pleads to me for life
With just demand, and I must grant it him:
My mistress she hath forced me with an oath,
For Susan's sake, the which I may not break,
For that is nearer than a master's love:
That grim-faced fellow, pitiless Black Will,
And Shakebag, stern in bloody stratagem,
—Two rougher ruffians never lived in Kent,—
Have sworn my death, if I infringe my vow,
A dreadful thing to be considered of.
Methinks I see them with their bolstered[48] hair
Staring and grinning in thy gentle face,
And in their ruthless hands their daggers drawn,
Insulting o'er thee with a peck of oaths,
Whilst thou submissive, pleading for relief,
Art mangled by their ireful instruments.
Methinks I hear them ask where Michael is,
And pitiless Black Will cries: "Stab the slave!
The peasant will detect[49] the tragedy!"
The wrinkles in his foul death-threat'ning face
Gapes open wide, like graves to swallow men.

....

[48]disheveled
[49]disclose

My death to him is but a merriment,
And he will murder me to make him sport.
He comes, he comes! ah, Master Franklin, help!
Call on the neighbors, or we are but dead!

#2 Male—Dramatic
Mosbie: a young man in over his head, 20s

Mosbie's affair with the passionate young wife of Master Arden has led to a wicked
scheme of murder. When Mosbie realizes how easy it was for Alice to plot to kill her
husband, he begins to worry about his own future.

MOSBIE: Disturbèd thoughts drives me from company
And dries my marrow with their watchfulness;
Continual trouble of my moody brain
Feebles my body by excess of drink,
And nips me as the bitter north-east wind
Doth check the tender blossoms in the spring.
Well fares the man, howe'er his cates[50] do taste,
That tables[51] not with foul suspicion;
And he but pines amongst his delicates,
Whose troubled mind is stuffed with discontent.
My golden time was when I had no gold;
Though then I wanted, yet I slept secure;
My daily toil begat me might's repose,
My night's repose made daylight fresh to me.
But since I climbed the top-bough of the tree
And sought to build my nest among the clouds,
Each gentle stirry[52] gale doth shake my bed,
And makes me dread my downfall to the earth.
But whither doth contemplation carry me?
The way I seek to find, where pleasure dwells,
Is hedged behind me that I cannot back,
But needs must on, although to danger's gate.
Then, Arden, perish thou by that decree;
For Greene doth ear[53] the land and weed thee up

---

[50]dainties
[51]dines
[52]stirring (active)[?]
[53]plow

To make my harvest nothing but pure corn.
And for his pains I'll hive him up a while,
And after smother him to have his wax:
Such bees as Greene must never live to sting.
Then is there Michael and the painter too,
Chief actors to Arden's overthrow;
Who when they shall see me sit in Arden's seat,
They will insult upon me for my meed,[54]
Or fright me by detecting of[55] his end.
I'll none of that, for I can cast a bone
To make these curs pluck out each other's throat,
And then am I sole ruler of mine own.
Yet Mistress Arden lives; but she's myself,
And holy Church rites makes us two but one.
But what for that? I may not trust you, Alice:
You have supplanted Arden for my sake,
And will extirpen[56] me to plant another.
'Tis fearful sleeping in a serpent's bed,
And I will cleanly rid my hands of her.

<hr />

[54]That is, They will assail me disrespectfully for my corrupt gain.
[55]revealing
[56]extirpate

The Atheist's Tragedy

Cyril Tourneur
1611

Scene: a banquet

Male—Dramatic
> Borachio: a scheming villain, 30–40

> Borachio's master is brother to a wealthy baron, whose estate Borachio covets. He
> has convinced his master to do away with his nephew, Charlemont, so that he will
> inherit the baron's estate. Here, Borachio dons a disguise and falsely informs the
> baron that Charlemont has been drowned.

BORACHIO: The enemy, defeated of a fair
Advantage by a flatt'ring[57] stratagem,
Plants all th'artillery against the town,
Whose thunder and lightning made our bulwarks shake;
And threat'ned in that terrible report
The storm wherewith they meant to second it.[58]
Th'assault was general. But for the place
That promis'd most advantage to be forc'd,
The pride of all their army was drawn forth,
And equally divided into front
And rear. They march'd. And coming to a stand,
Ready to pass our channel at an ebb,[59]
W'advis'd it for our safest course, to draw
Our sluices up and make't unpassable.
Our governor oppos'd; and suffer'd 'em
To charge us home e'en to the rampier's[60] foot,
But when their front was forcing up our breach,
At push o'pike,[61] then did his policy
Let go the sluices, and tripp'd up the heels
Of the whole body of their troop, that stood

---

[57]deceptive
[58]follow it up
[59]The river of course is tidal.
[60]rampart
[61]in hand-to-hand combat

Within the violent current of the stream.
Their front beleaguer'd 'twixt the water and
The town, seeing the flood was grown too deep
To promise them a safe retreat, expos'd
The force of all their spirits, (like the last
Expiring gasp of a strong-hearted man)
Upon the hazard of one charge; but were
Oppress'd and fell. The rest that could not swim
Were only drown'd; but those that thought to scape
By swimming were, by murtherers that flanker'd
The level of the flood,[62] both drown'd and slain.
[*D'AMVILLE:* Now by my soul (soldier) a brave service.]
[*MONTFERRERS:* O what became of my dear Charlemont?]
BORACHIO: Walking next day upon the fatal shore,
Among the slaughter'd bodies of their men,
Which the full-stomach'd sea had cast upon
The sands, it was m'unhappy chance to light
Upon a face, whose favour when it liv'd
My astonish'd mind inform'd me I had seen.
He lay in's armour, as if that had been
His coffin; and the weeping sea, (like one
Whose milder temper doth lament the death
Of him whom in his rage he slew) runs up
The shore; embraces him; kisses his cheek,
Goes back again and forces up the sands
To bury him; and ev'ry time it parts,
Sheds tears upon him; till at last (as if
It could no longer endure to see the man
Whom it had slain, yet loath to leave him,) with
A kind of unresolv'd unwilling pace,
Winding her waves one in another, like
A man that folds his arms, or wrings his hands
For grief; ebb'd from the body and descends;
As if it would sink down into the earth,
And hide it self for shame of such a deed.

---

[62]spread along the banks

[*D'AMVILLE:* And souldier, who was this?]
[*MONTFERRERS:* O Charlemont!]
BORACHIO: Your fear hath told you that whereof my grief
Was loath to be the messenger.

Bartholomew Fair

Ben Jonson
1614

Scene: the Bartholomew Fair

Male—Serio-Comic
    Quarlous: a gamester, 30–40

    Here, the rascally Quarlous chides a friend for his habit of romancing older women.

QUARLOUS: Hoy-day! How respective[63] you are become o' the sudden! I fear this family will turn you reformed too; pray you come about again. Because she is in possibility to be your daughter-in-law, and may ask you blessing hereafter, when she courts it to Tottenham[64] to eat cream—well, I will forbear, sir; but i' faith, would thou wouldst leave thy exercise of widow-hunting once, this drawing after[65] an old reverend smock by the splay-foot! There cannot be an ancient tripe or trillibub[66] i' the town, but thou art straight nosing it; and 'tis a fine occupation[67] thou'lt confine thyself to, when thou has got one—scrubbing piece of buff,[68] as if thou hadst the perpetuity of Pannyer-alley[69] to stink in, or perhaps, worse, currying[70] a carcass that thou hast bound thyself to alive. I'll be sworn, some of them, that thou art or hast been a suitor to, are so old as no chaste or married pleasure can ever become 'em: the honest instrument of procreation has, forty years since, left to belong to 'em; thou must visit 'em, as thou wouldst do a tomb, with a torch, or three handfuls of link,[71] flaming hot, and so thou mayst hap to make 'em feel thee, and after, come to inherit according to thy inches. A sweet course for a man to waste the brand of life for, to be still raking himself a fortune in an old woman's embers; we shall ha' thee, after

----

[63]careful (of manners)
[64]Probably Tottenham Court, like Hoston (I.ii.6.n), a favorite place to buy cakes and cream.
[65]tracking by the scent
[66]The entrails; also a jeering name for a fat man (Grose).
[67]Probably a play on *occupy*, have sexual intercourse with (cf. Ep., 117).
[68]Leather; bare skin ("Stripped to the buff").
[69]An alley out of Pater Noster Row; connected with either the selling or making of leather.
[70]rubbing down (a horse)
[71]torch made of tow and pitch

thou hast been but a month married to one of 'em, look like the quartan ague[72] and the black jaundice[73] met in a face, and walk as if thou hadst borrow'd legs of a spinner,[74] and voice of a cricket. I would endure to hear fifteen sermons a week 'fore[75] her, and such coarse and loud ones as some of 'em must be; I would e'en desire of Fate, I might dwell in a drum, and take in my sustenance with an old broken tobacco-pipe and a straw. Dost thou ever think to bring thine ears or stomach to the patience of a dry[76] grace, as long as thy tablecloth, and dron'd out by the son here, that might be thy father, till all the meat o' thy board has forgot it was that day i' the kitchen? Or to brook the noise made, in a question of predestination, by the good laborers and painful eaters assembled together, put to 'em by the matron, your spouse, who moderates with a cup of wine, ever and anon, and a sentence out of Knox between? Or the perpetual spitting, before and after a sober drawn[77] exhortation of six hours, whose better part was the hum-ha-hum? Or to hear prayers groan'd out, over thy iron-chests, as if they were charms to break 'em? And all this, for the hope of two apostle-spoons,[78] to suffer! And a cup to eat a caudle[79] in! For that will be thy legacy. She'll ha' convey'd her state,[80] safe enough from thee, an' she be a right widow.

---

[72]Fever in which a paroxysm occurs every fourth day.

[73]Caused by obstruction of the bile and called black or yellow according to the resulting color of the skin.

[74]spider

[75]in preference to

[76]Plain; thirsty (Puritans favored very long graces before meals).

[77]drawn out

[78]Silver, with the figure of an apostle on the handle, a common present of sponsors at baptism; since genuine Puritans would be likely to consider such presents profane, Dame Purecraft's devotion seems spurious.

[79]a warm concoction for sick persons

[80]made her estate over to another

Cambyses, King of Persia
Thomas Preston
1569–70

Scene: Persia

Male—Serio-Comic
> Ambidexter: the Vice, 30–40

> The crafty Ambidexter has wormed his way into the court of Cambyses by playing all sides against one another. Here, he takes a moment to speak out against marriage.

AMBIDEXTER: Oh the passion of me! Marry, as ye say, yonder is a
  royal court.
There is triumphing and sport upon sport,
Such loyal lords, with such lordly exercise,
Frequenting such pastime as they can devise,
Running at tilt, jousting, with running at the ring,[81]
Masking and mumming with each kind of thing,
Such dancing, such singing, with musical harmony.
Believe me, I was loath to absent their company.
But will you believe? Jesu, what haste thay made till they were married!
Not for a million of pounds one day longer they would have tarried.
O, there was a banquet royal and super-excellent!
Thousands and thousands at that banquet was spent.
I muse of nothing but how they can be married so soon.
I care not if I be married before tomorrow at noon,
If marriage be a thing that so may be had.
(*To a girl in the audience.*) How say you, maid? To marry me will ye be
  glad?—
Out of doubt, I believe it is some excellent treasure;
Else to the same belongs abundant pleasure.
Yet with mine ears I have heard some say,
"That ever I was married, now cursèd be the day!"
Those be they (that)[82] with curst[83] wives be matched.
That husband for hawk's meat[84] of[85] them is up-snatched,

---

[81]Trying to catch a ring on the end of a lance.
[82]From Q2, not in Q1.
[83]shrewish

Head broke with a bedstaff,[86] face all-to bescratched—
"Knave!" "Slave!" and "Villain!"—a coiled coat[87] now and then.
When the wife hath given it, she will say, "Alas, good man!"
Such were better unmarried, my masters, I trow,
Than all their life after be matchèd with a shrew.

---

[84]Something snatched greedily.
[85]by
[86]Slat for mattress.
[87]beating

Catiline

Ben Jonson
1611

Scene: Rome

#1 Male—Dramatic
    Sylla: ghost of a Roman dictator, 50–60

> As the unhappy spirit of the murdered Sylla wanders the palace, he encounters the treacherous Catiline, who is in the process of planning a deadly coup.

SYLLA'S GHOST: Dost thou not feel me, Rome? Not yet? Is night
So heavy on thee, and my weight so light?
Can Sylla's ghost arise within thy walls
Less threat'ning than an earthquake, the quick falls
Of thee and thine? Shake not the frighted heads
Of thy steep[88] towers, or shrink to their first beds,
Or, as their ruin[89] the large Tiber fills,
Make that swell up and drown thy seven proud hills?
What sleep is this doth seize thee, so like death
And is not it? Wake, feel her in my breath;
Behold, I come, sent from the Stygian sound
As a dire vapor that had cleft the ground
T'engender with the night and blast the day,
Or like a pestilence that should display[90]
Infection through the world, which thus I do.
(*Discovers[91] Catiline in his study.*)
Pluto be at thy counsels, and into
Thy darker bosom enter Sylla's spirit:
All that was mine, and bad, thy breast inherit.
Alas, how weak is that for Catiline!
Did I but say—vain voice!—all that was mine?
All that the Gracchi, Cinna, Marius would;
What now, had I a body again, I could,
Coming from hell; what fiends would wish should be,

....

[88]lofty
[89]collapse
[90]spread
[91]reveals

And Hannibal could not have wish'd to see;
Think thou, and practice.[92] Let the long-hid seeds
Of treason in thee now shoot forth in deeds
Ranker than horror, and thy former facts[93]
Not fall in mention,[94] but[95] to urge new acts.
Conscience[96] of them provoke thee on to more.
Be still thy incests, murders, rapes before
Thy sense:[97] thy forcing[98] first a Vestal nun,[99]
Thy parricide,[100] late, on thine own only son,
After his mother, to make empty way
For thy last wicked nuptials; worse than they
That blaze,[101] that act of thy incestuous life
Which got thee at once a daughter and a wife.
I leave[102] the slaughters that thou didst for me
Of Senators,[103] for which I hid for thee
Thy murder of thy brother, being so brib'd,
And writ him in the list of my proscrib'd
After thy fact, to save thy little shame;
Thy incest with thy sister, I not name.
These are too light. Fate will have thee pursue
Deeds after which no mischief[104] can be new,
The ruin of thy country; thou wert built
For such a work, and born for no less guilt.
What though defeated[105] once th'hast been, and known,[106]
Tempt[107] it again: that is thy act, or none.

---

[92]carry out
[93]crimes
[94]be mentioned (Lat. *in mentionem incidere*)
[95]except
[96]consciousness
[97]let . . . remain in your awareness
[98]raping
[99]Cicero's wife's sister, according to Asconius 82.
[100]Murder of a close relative (not necessarily a father).
[101]flagrant crime
[102]pass over
[103]The ancient sources specify only *equites*, knights.
[104]cause of evil
[105]In the alleged conspiracy of 66/65 B.C.
[106]discovered
[107]attempt

What all the several ills that visit earth,
Brought forth by night with a sinister birth,
Plagues, famine, fire could not reach unto,
The sword, no surfeits, let thy fury do:
Make all past, present, future ill thine own,
And conquer all example[108] in thy one,
Nor let thy thought find any vacant time
To hate an old, but still a fresher crime
Drown the remembrance; let not mischief cease
But while it is in punishing, increase.
Conscience and care die in thee, and be free
Not heav'n itself from thy impiety.[109]
Let night grow blacker with thy plots, and day,
At showing but thy head forth, start away
From this half-sphere, and leave Rome's blinded walls
T'embrace lusts, hatreds, slaughters, funerals,
And not recover sight till their own flames
Do light them to their ruins. All the names
Of thy confederates, too, be no less great
In hell than here, that when we would repeat
Our strengths in muster, we may name you all,
And Furies upon you, for Furies, call;
Whilst what you do may strike them into fears,
Or make them grieve and wish your mischief theirs.

#2 Male—Dramatic
    Cicero: Roman statesman and orator, 40s

    Having discovered the evil Catiline's plot to overthrow the empire, Cicero here
    muses over those who have attempted similar feats.

CICERO: Is there a heaven, and gods, and can it be
They should so slowly hear, so slowly see?
Hath Jove no thunder, or is Jove become
Stupid[110] as thou art, O near-wretched Rome,
When both thy Senate and thy gods do sleep

....

[108]Outdo all similar deeds.
[109]Lack of dutiful attitude.
[110]torpid

And neither thine nor their own states do keep?
What will awake thee, heaven, what can excite
Thine anger if this practice be too light?[111]
His former drifts[112] partake[113] of former times,
But this last plot was only Catiline's.
O that it were his last, but he before
Hath safely done so much, he'll still dare more.
Ambition, like a torrent, ne'er looks back,
And is a swelling[114] and the last affection
A high mind can put off, being both a rebel
Unto the soul and reason, and enforceth[115]
All laws, all conscience, treads upon religion
And offereth violence to nature's self.
But here is that transcends it: a black purpose
To confound[116] nature and to ruin that
Which never age[117] nor mankind can repair.
Sit down, good lady; Cicero is lost
In this your fable, for to think it true
Tempteth[118] my reason, it so far exceeds
All insolent fictions of the tragic scene:[119]
The Commonwealth yet panting underneath
The stripes[120] and wounds of a late civil war,
Gasping for life, and scarce restor'd to hope;
To seek t'oppress her with new cruelty
And utterly extinguish her long[121] name
With so prodigious and unheard-of fierceness!
What sink[122] of monsters, wretches of lost minds
Mad after change and desp'rate in their states,

---

[111]trivial
[112]plots
[113]Have the qualities.
[114]increasing
[115]Overcomes by force.
[116]Cast into confusion.
[117]time
[118]tests
[119]unusual (Lat. *insolens*) . . . stage tragedies
[120]strokes
[121]ancient
[122]Place where vice collects.

Wearied and gall'd[123] with their necessities,
For all this I allow them, durst have thought it?
Would not the barbarous deeds have been believ'd
Of Marius and Sylla by our children
Without this fact had rise forth greater for them?[124]
All that they did was piety to[125] this:
They yet but murder'd kinsfolk, brothers, parents,
Ravish'd the virgins and, perhaps, some matrons.
They left the city standing, and the temples;
The gods and majesty of Rome were safe yet.
These purpose to fire it, to despoil them,
Beyond the other evils, and lay waste
The far-triumphed[126] world, for unto whom
Rome[127] is too little, what can be enough?

. . . .

[123]chafed
[124]Unless the even greater atrocity had appeared to confirm the lesser.
[125]compared with
[126]Over which victories had been won far and wide, and celebrated with triumphs at Rome.
[127]"There is a pun on 'Rome' and 'room' similarly pronounced . . . *Julius Caesar*, I.ii.157–8" (H & S).

Cymbeline

William Shakespeare
1610

Scene: Britain

Male—Dramatic
   Posthumus: a gentleman, married to Imogen, 30s

Posthumus has been tricked into believing that his wife has been unfaithful. In a
rage, he orders his servant, Pisanio, to murder her. Fortunately Pisano is unable to
carry out his master's orders and takes Imogene to Wales, instead. In the meantime,
Posthumus has joined with the Roman army that now threatens Britain. Here, the
unhappy man grieves for the wife he believes is dead.

POSTHUMUS: Yea, bloody cloth, I'll keep thee, for I wish'd
Thou shouldst be colour'd thus. You married ones,
If each of you should take this course, how many
Must murder wives much better than themselves
For wrying but a little! O Pisanio!
Every good servant does not all commands:
No bond but to do just ones. God! if you
Should have ta'en vengeance on my faults, I never
Had lived to put on this: so had you saved
The noble Imogen to repent and struck
Me, wretch more worth your vengeance. But, alack,
You snatch some hence for little faults: that's love,
To have them fall no more: you some permit
To second ills with ills, each elder worse,
And make them dread it, to the doers' thrift.
But Imogen is your own: do your best wills,
And make me the blest to obey! I am brought hither
Among the Italian gentry, and to fight
Against my lady's kingdom: 'tis enough
That, Britain, I have kill'd thy mistress; peace!
I'll give no wound to thee. Therefore, good heavens,
Hear patiently my purpose: I'll disrobe me
Of these Italian weeds and suit myself
As does a Briton peasant: so I'll fight
Against the part I come with; so I'll die

For thee, O Imogen, even for whom my life
Is every breath a death; and thus, unknown,
Pitied nor hated, to the face of peril
Myself I'll dedicate. Let me make men know
More valour in me than my habits show.
Gods, put the strength o' the Leonati in me!
To shame the guise o' the world, I will begin
The fashion, less without and more within.

David and Bethsabe

George Peele
1599

Scene: Israel

Male–Dramatic
David: King of Israel, 40s

David's son, Absalon, has murdered his brother, Amnon. Here, the grieving king leads his people in mourning the loss of his son.

DAVID: Proud lust, the bloodiest traitor to our souls,
Whose greedy throat nor earth, air, sea, or heaven,
Can glut or satisfy with any store,
Thou art the cause these torments suck my blood,
Piercing with venom of thy poisoned eyes
The strength and marrow of my tainted bones.
To punish Pharaoh and his cursèd host,
The waters shrunk[128] at great Adonai's voice,
And sandy bottom of the sea appeared,
Offering his service at his servant's feet;
And, to inflict a plague on David's sin,
He makes his bowels traitors to his breast,
Winding about his heart with mortal gripes.[129]
Ah, Absalon, the wrath of heaven inflames
Thy scorchèd bosom with ambitious heat,
And Satan sets thee on a lusty[130] tower,
Showing thy thoughts the pride of Israel,
Of choice to cast thee on her ruthless stones.—
Weep with me, then, ye sons of Israel;
(*Lies down, and all the rest after him.*)
Lie down with David, and with David mourn
Before the Holy One that sees our hearts;
Season this heavy soil with showers of tears,
And fill the face of every flower with dew;

....

[128]shrinke Q
[129]grip
[130]of lust

Weep, Israel, for David's soul dissolves,
Lading[131] the fountains of his drownèd eyes,
And pours her substance on the senseless earth.

---

[131]draining

Doctor Faustus

Christopher Marlowe
1588–93

Scene: Germany

Male—Dramatic
  Faustus: a doctor obsessed with the black arts, 30–40

As he prepares to summon the evil spirits that will reveal to him the secrets of necromancy, Faustus fantasizes about the many feats that he will command the spirits to perform.

FAUSTUS: How am I glutted with conceit of this![132]
Shall I make spirits fetch me what I please,
Resolve me of all ambiguities,
Perform what desperate enterprise I will?
I'll have them fly to India for gold,
Ransack the ocean for orient pearl,
And search all corners of the new-found world
For pleasant fruits and princely delicates;[133]
I'll have them read me strange philosophy,
And tell the secrets of all foreign kings;
I'll have them wall all Germany with brass,
And make swift Rhine circle fair Wittenberg.
I'll have them fill the public schools[134] with silk,
Wherewith the students shall be bravely[135] clad;
I'll levy soldiers with the coin they bring,
And chase the Prince of Parma[136] from our land,
And reign sole king of all the Provinces;
Yea, stranger engines for the brunt[137] of war,
Than was the fiery keel at Antwerpe bridge,[138]
I'll make my servile spirits to invent.
(*He calls within. Enter VALDES and CORNELIUS.*)

---

[132]this notion
[133]delicacies
[134]university lecture rooms
[135]handsomely
[136]Spanish governor-general of the Netherlands (1579–92).
[137]violence
[138]A Dutch fire-ship used to damage Parma's bridge over the Scheldt river in April 1585.

Come, German Valdes, and Cornelius,
And make me blest with your sage conference!
Valdes, sweet Valdes, and Cornelius,
Know that your words have won me at the last
To practise magic and concealed arts:
Yet not your words only, but mine own fantasy,[139]
That will receive no object,[140] for my head
But ruminates on necromantic skill.
Philosophy is odious and obscure;
Both law and physic are for petty wits;
Divinity is basest of the three,[141]
Unpleasant, harsh, contemptible, and vile:
'Tis magic, magic, that hath ravish'd me.
Then, gentle friends, aid me in this attempt
And I, that have with subtle syllogisms
Gravell'd[142] the pastors of the German church,
And made the flowering pride of Wittenberg
Swarm to my problems,[143] as the infernal spirits
On sweet Musæus[144] when he came to hell,
Will be as cunning as Agrippa[145] was,
Whose shadows made all Europe honour him.

---

[139]imagination
[140]Usual academic subject.
[141]baser than the others
[142]confounded
[143]lectures
[144]Pre-Homeric Greek poet. See *Aeneid*, vi, 667.
[145]Henry Cornelius Agrippa von Nettesheim, Renaissance magician thought to have the power of calling up the shadows of the dead.

The Dutch Courtesan

John Marston
1603

Scene: London

#1 Male—Serio-Comic
   Freevill: an unscrupulous young man, 20–30

   Here, Freevill defends the right of women to prostitute themselves when the need
   arises.

FREEVILL: Alas, good creatures, what would you have them do?
Would you have them get their living by the curse of man, the sweat of
their brows? So they do. Every man must follow his trade, and every
woman her occupation. A poor, decayed mechanical man's[146] wife, her
husband is laid up; may not she lawfully be laid down when her
husband's only rising is by his wife's falling? A captain's wife wants
means, her commander lies in open field abroad; may not she lie in civil
arms[147] at home? A waiting gentlewoman, that had wont to take say[148]
to her lady, miscarries or so,[149] the court misfortune throws her down;
may not the city courtesy take her up? Do you know no alderman
would pity such a woman's case?[150] Why is charity grown a sin? or
relieving the poor and impotent an offense? You will say beasts take no
money for their fleshly entertainment. True, because they are beasts,
therefore beastly: only men give to loose[151] because they are men,
therefore manly; and, indeed, wherein should they bestow their money
better? In land, the title may be crack'd; in houses, they may be burnt;
in apparel, 'twill wear; in wine, alas for pity, our throat is but short. But
employ your money upon women, and, a thousand to nothing, some
one of them will bestow that on you which shall stick by you as long as
you live. They are no ingrateful persons; they will give *quid* for *quo*:[152]

....

[146]Manual worker's, handicraftsman's.
[147]A play on *civil* as citizen's or civilian's (as opposed to soldier's or military) and *civil* as
the opposite of *uncivil*.
[148]A pun on *say*, a fine serge-like cloth, and *say*, the action of testing (see *OED*). The
waiting-woman has sampled her lady's lovers, become pregnant, and been turned out of
her post.
[149]Or something of that kind—emphasizing the pun in *miscarries*.
[150]"A play on words: (1) case; (2) *kaze* (= *pudendum muliebre*)" (*Bullen*).
[151]Loose living, indulgence.

do ye protest, they'll swear; do you rise, they'll fall; do you fall, they'll rise; do you give them the French crown, they'll give you the French[153]—*O justus justa justum!*[154] They sell their bodies; do not better persons sell their souls?[155] Nay, since all things have been sold—honor, justice, faith, nay, even God himself—

Ay me, what base ignobleness is it
To sell the pleasure of a wanton bed?
Why do men scrape,[156] why heap to full heaps join?
But for his mistress, who would care for coin?
For this I hold to be denied of no man:
All things are made for man, and man for woman.
Give me my fee![157]

#2 Male—Serio-Comic
     Cocledemoy: a knavishly witty companion, 30–40

     During an evening of revelry, Cocledemoy takes a moment to raise his glass in salute to an old bawd.

COCLEDEMOY: Hang toasts![158] I rail at thee, my worshipful organ-bellows that fills the pipes, my fine rattling, phlegmy[159] cough o' the lungs and cold with a pox?[160] I rail at thee? What, my right precious pandress, supportress of barber-surgeons[161] and enhanceress[162] of lotium[163] and diet-drink![164] I rail at thee, necessary damnation?[165] I'll make an oration, I, in praise of thy most courtly-in-fashion and most

---

[152]tit for tat

[153]Pox (understood); a word-play on the fact that the French crown, the coin of Henri IV of France, having the figure of the king's head on the obverse side, was also in England the jocular name for the baldness produced by the *French pox*, or venereal disease.

[154]Declension of the Latin adjective *justus* (just).

[155]See Appendix A.

[156]amass (wealth)

[157]Freevill, laughingly, asks for a fee as a lawyer who has just concluded a speech for the defense of his client (the courtesan). Cf. Cocledemoy's parallel conclusion to his praise of bawds in the next scene (l. 54).

[158]Cocledemoy's favorite exclamanation. Spiced toasts dropped in liquor were a favorite treat at this time.

[159]watery

[160]syphilis

[161]The two professions were united in one guild.

[162]One who "enhances" or raises the price.

[163]Stale urine, used by barbers as "lye" for the hair (*OED*).

[164]"To take diet" is to be treated for the pox.

[165]damned person

pleasurable function, I.

[*MARY FAUGH:* I prithee do; I love to hear myself prais'd, as well as any old lady, I.]

COCLEDEMOY: List, then: a bawd, first for her profession or vocation, it is most worshipful of all the twelve companies,[166] for as that trade is most honorable that sells the best commodities—as the draper[167] is more worshipful than the pointmaker,[168] the silkman more worshipful than the draper, and the goldsmith more honorable than both, little Mary—so the bawd above all. Her shop has the best ware; for where these sell but cloth, satins, and jewels, she sells divine virtues as virginity, modesty, and such rare gems, and those not like a petty chapman,[169] by retail, but like a great merchant, by wholesale. Wa, ha, ho![170] And who are her customers? Not base corn-cutters[171] or sowgelders, but most rare wealthy knights and most rare bountiful lords are her customers. Again, whereas no trade or vocation profiteth but by the loss and displeasure of another—as the merchant thrives not but by the licentiousness of giddy and unsettled youth, the lawyer but by the vexation of his client, the physician but by the maladies of his patient—only my smooth-gumm'd bawd lives by others' pleasure, and only grows rich by others' rising.[172] O merciful gain! O righteous income! So much for her vocation, trade, and life. As for their death, how can it be bad since their wickedness is always before their eyes, and a death's head[173] most commonly on their middle finger? To conclude, 'tis most certain they must needs both live well and die well since most commonly they live in Clerkenwell[174] and die in Bridewell.[175] *Dixi*,[176] Mary.

---

[166]The twelve major London trade companies (the Livery Guilds): the mercers, grocers, drapers, fishmongers, goldsmiths, skinners, merchant tailors, haberdashers, salters, ironmongers, vintners, clothworkers.

[167]A maker of woolen cloth.

[168]A maker of points or laces (for fastening apparel) (*OED*).

[169]retail dealer

[170]The cry of the falconer to lure the falcon.

[171]chiropodists

[172]See Appendix A.

[173]A ring with the figure of a skull, commonly worn by procuresses at this time.

[174]A district in London notorious as a haunt of thieves and loose women.

[175]A house of correction. Cocledemoy's formal praise of the bawd should be compared with Freevill's formal praise of the courtesan in the preceding scene.

[176]"I have spoken" or "I have presented my case"; a legal term, with which a Roman praetor concluded a speech to indicate that he had pronounced judgment.

Edward II

Christopher Marlowe
1591–92

Scene: Kenilworth Castle, England

Male—Dramatic
> King Edward: a monarch held prisoner by usurping lords, 30–40

> Edward is a weak and foolish king whose flamboyant ways have earned him nothing but scorn from many earls attending the court. This animosity finally leads to rebellion and Edward is taken to Kenilworth Castle where he is held prisoner. Edward has long suspected that his wife, Queen Isabella, has been having an affair with young Lord Mortimer, the leader of the coup, and here laments his fate to the Earl of Leicester.

KING EDWARD: Leicester, if gentle words might comfort me,
Thy speeches long ago had eased my sorrows;
For kind and loving hast thou always been.
The griefs of private men are soon allayed,
But not of kings. The forest deer, being struck,
Runs to an herb[177] that closeth up the wounds;
but, when the imperial lion's flesh is gored,
He rends and tears it with his wrathful paw,
And highly scorning that the lowly earth
Should drink his blood, mounts up to the air.
And so it fares with me, whose dauntless mind
The ambitious Mortimer would seek to curb,
And that unnatural queen, false Isabel,
That thus hath pent and mewed[178] me in a prison;
For such outrageous passions cloy my soul,
As with the wings of rancour and disdain,
Full often am I soaring up to Heaven,
To plain[179] me to the gods against them both.
But when I call to mind I am a king,
Methinks I should revenge me of my wrongs,
That Mortimer and Isabel have done.

....

[177]dittany
[178]shut
[179]complain

But what are kings, when regiment[180] is gone,
But perfect shadows in a sunshine[181] day?
My nobles rule, I bear the name of king;
I wear the crown, but am controlled by them,
By Mortimer, and my unconstant queen,
Who spots my nuptial bed with infamy;
Whilst I am lodged within this cave of care,
Where sorrow at my elbow still attends,
To company my heart with sad laments,
That bleeds within me for this strange exchange.
But tell me, must I now resign my crown,
To make usurping Mortimer a king?
[*BISHOP OF WINCHESTER:* Your grace mistakes; it is for England's
    good,
And princely Edward's right we crave the crown.]
KING EDWARD: No, 'tis for Mortimer, not Edward's head;
For he's a lamb, encompassèd by wolves,
Which in a moment will abridge his life.
But if proud Mortimer do wear this crown,
Heavens turn it to a place of quenchless fire
Or like the snaky wreath of Tisiphon,[182]
Engirt the temples of his hateful head;
So shall not England's vine be perishèd,
But Edward's name survives, though Edward dies.
[*LEICESTER:* My lord, why waste you thus the time away?
They stay your answer; will you yield your crown?]
KING EDWARD: Ah, Leicester, weigh how hardly I can brook
To lose my crown and kingdom without cause;
To give ambitious Mortimer my right,
That like a mountain overwhelms my bliss,
In which extreme my mind here murdered is.
But what the heavens appoint, I must obey!
Here, take my crown; the life of Edward too;
(*Taking off the crown.*)

---

[180]rule
[181]sunny
[182]Tisiphone, a Fury.

Two kings of England cannot reign at once.
But stay awhile, let me be king till night,
That I may gaze upon this glittering crown;
So shall my eyes receive their last content,
My head, the latest honour due to it,
And jointly both yield up their wishèd right.
Continue ever thou celestial sun;
Let never silent night possess this clime;
Stand still you watches of the element;[183]
All times and seasons, rest you at a stay,
That Edward may be still fair England's king!
But day's bright beam doth vanish fast away,
And needs I must resign my wishèd crown.
Inhuman creatures! nursed with tiger's milk!
Why gape you for your sovereign's overthrow!
My diadem I mean, and guiltless life.
See, monsters, see, I'll wear my crown again!
(*He puts on the crown.*)
What, fear you not the fury of your king?
But, hapless Edward, thou art fondly[184] led;
They pass[185] not for thy frown as late they did,
But seek to make a new-elected king;
Which fills my mind with strange despairing thoughts,
Which thoughts are martyrèd with endless torments,
And in this torment comfort find I none,
But that I feel the crown upon my head;
And therefore let me wear it awhile.

[183]That is, heavenly bodies.
[184]foolishly
[185]care

Epiocene or The Silent Woman

Ben Jonson

1609

Scene: London

#1 Male—Serio-Comic
   Sir Amorous La-Foole: a knight, 30–40

   La-Foole—a talkative and foolish man—here invites some friends to dinner while
   offering at the same time a history of his family.

LA-FOOLE: No, sir, the La-Fooles of London.

[*CLERIMONT: (Aside.)* Now, h' is in.]

LA-FOOLE: They all come out of our house, the La-Fooles o' the north,
the La-Fooles of the west, the La-Fooles of the east and south—we are
as ancient a family as any is in Europe—but I myself am descended
lineally of the French La-Fooles—and, we do bear for our coat[186]
yellow, or *or*, checker'd *azure*, and *gules*,[187] and some three or four
colours more, which is a very noted coat, and has, sometimes, been
solemnly worn by divers nobility of our house—but let that go, antiq-
uity is not respected now.—I had a brace of fat does sent me,
gentlemen, and half a dozen of pheasants, a dozen or two of
godwits,[188] and some other fowl, which I would have eaten, while they
are good, and in good company:—there will be a great lady or two, my
lady Haughty, my lady Centaure, mistress Dol Mavis—and they come
o' purpose to see the silent gentlewoman, mistress Epicone, that honest
Sir John Daw has promis'd to bring thither—and then, mistress Trusty,
my lady's woman, will be there too, and this honourable knight, Sir
Dauphine, with yourself, master Clerimont—and we'll be very merry,
and have fiddlers, and dance.—I have been a mad wag in my time, and
have spent some crowns since I was a page in court, to my lord Lofty,
and after, my lady's gentleman-usher, who got me knighted in Ireland,
since it pleas'd my elder brother to die.—I had as fair a gold jerkin on
that day, as any worn in the Island Voyage,[189] or at Caliz,[190] none

....

[186]coat of arms
[187]red
[188]marsh birds

disprais'd: and I came over in it hither, show'd myself to my friends in court, and after went down to my tenants in the country, and survey'd my lands, let new leases, took their money, spent it in the eye o' the land[191] here, upon ladies:—and now I can take up at my pleasure.

#2 Male—Serio-Comic
Truewit: a friend of Morose, a gentleman who loves no noise, 40s

Morose has decided to marry to prevent his nephew from enjoying his inheritance. Here, his friend Truewit does his best to discourage him.

TRUEWIT: Alas, sir, I am but a messenger: I but tell you, what you must hear. It seems your friends are careful after your soul's health, sir, and would have you know the danger: (but you may do your pleasure for all them, I persuade not, sir.) If, after you are married, your wife do run away with a vaulter, or the Frenchman that walks upon ropes, or him that dances the jig, or a fencer for his skill at his weapon; why it is not their fault, they have discharged their consciences, when you know what may happen. Nay, suffer valiantly, sir, for I must tell you all the perils that you are obnoxious[192] to. If she be fair, young and vege-tous,[193] no sweetmeats ever drew more flies; all the yellow doublets and great roses[194] i' the town will be there. If foul and crooked, she'll be with them, and buy those doublets and roses, sir. If rich, and that you marry her dowry, not her, she'll reign in your house as imperious as a widow. If noble, all her kindred will be your tyrants. If fruitful, as proud as May, and humorous[195] as April; she must have her doctors, her midwives, her nurses, her longings every hour; though it be for the dearest morsel of man. If learned, there was never such a parrot; all your patrimony will be too little for the guests that must be invited to hear her speak Latin and Greek; and you must lie with her in those languages too, if you will please her. If precise,[196] you must feast all the silenc'd brethren,[197] once in three days; salute the sisters; entertain the

----

[189]Against the Azores, in 1597.
[190]Cadiz, attacked and captured by the English fleet in 1596.
[191]London
[192]liable
[193]active
[194]I.e., gallants. Roses were ornaments on shoes.
[195]changeable

whole family, or wood[198] of 'em; and hear long-winded exercises,
singings and catechizings, which you are not given to, and yet must
give for; to please the zealous matron your wife, who for the holy
cause, will cozen you over and above. You begin to sweat, sir! but this
is not half, i' faith: you may do your pleasure, notwithstanding, as I
said before: I come not to persuade you. (*The Mute is stealing away.*) —
Upon my faith, master serving-man, if you do stir, I will beat you.
[*MOROSE:* O, what is my sin! what is my sin!]
TRUEWIT: Then, if you love your wife, or rather dote on her, sir; O,
how she'll torture you, and take pleasure i' your torments! you shall lie
with her but when she lists; she will not hurt her beauty, her
complexion; or it must be for that jewel, or that pearl, when she does:
every half hour's pleasure must be bought anew, and with the same
pain and charge you woo'd her at first. Then you must keep what
servants she please; what company she will; that friend must not visit
you without her license; and him she loves most, she will seem to hate
eagerliest, to decline[199] your jealousy; or feign to be jealous of you first;
and for that cause go live with her she-friend, or cousin at the college,
that can instruct her in all the mysteries of writing letters, corrupting
servants, taming spies; where she must have that rich gown for such a
great day; a new one for the next; a richer for the third; be serv'd in
silver;[200] have the chamber fill'd with a succession of grooms, footmen,
ushers, and other messengers; besides embroiderers, jewellers, tire-
women,[201] sempsters, feathermen, perfumers; while she feels not how
the land drops away, nor the acres melt; nor forsees the change when
the mercer has your woods for her velvets; never weighs what her
pride costs, sir; so she may kiss a page, or a smooth chin, that has the
despair of a beard: be a stateswoman, know all the news, what was
done at Salisbury, what at the Bath, what at court, what in progress;[202]
or, so she may censure[203] poets and authors, and styles, and compare
'em; Daniel with Spenser, Jonson with the t' other youth, and so forth;

[196]puritanical
[197]Puritan clergy who had been deprived of their licenses to preach.
[198]crowd
[199]avert
[200]I.e., silver dishes.
[201]dressmakers

or be thought cunning in controversies, or the very knots of divinity; and have often in her mouth the state of the question;[204] and then skip to the mathematics, and demonstration: and answer in religion to one, in state to another, in bawdry to a third.

Every Man in His Humor

Ben Jonson
1598

Scene: London

Male—Serio-Comic
    Knowell: an older gentleman prying into his son's affairs, 50–60

> Knowell's son has received a mysterious letter from someone in the Jewery. Knowell managed to intercept and read the letter before it was delivered, and has therefore learned of his son's intention to visit the writer of the letter. Deciding to follow at a distance, the older man reflects on the differences between their generations and on the responsibility of fathers to their sons.

Knowell: I cannot lose the thought yet of this letter,
Sent to my son; not leave t' admire the change
Of manners, and the breeding of our youth
Within the kingdom, since myself was one.—
When I was young, he lived not in the stews
Durst have conceived a scorn, and utter'd it,
On a gray head; age was authority
Against a buffoon, and a man had then
A certain reverence paid unto his years,
That had none due unto his life: so much
The sanctity of some prevail'd for others.
But not we all are fallen; youth, from their fear,
And age, from that which bred it, good example.
Nay, would ourselves were not the first, even parents,
That did destroy the hopes in our own children;
Or they not learn'd our vices in their cradles,
And suck'd in our ill customs with their milk;
Ere all their teeth be born, or they can speak,
We make their palates cunning; the first words
We form their tongues with, are licentious jests:
Can it call whore? cry bastard? O, then, kiss it!
A witty child! can't swear? the father's darling!
Give it two plums. Nay, rather than't shall learn
No bawdy song, the mother herself will teach it!—
But this is in the infancy, the days

Of the long coat; when it puts on the breeches,
It will put off all this: Ay, it is like,
When it is gone into the bone already!
No, no; this dye goes deeper than the coat,
Or shirt, or skin; it stains into the liver,
And heart, in some; and rather than it should not,
Note what we fathers do! look how we live!
What mistresses we keep! at what expense,
In our sons' eyes! where they may handle our gifts,
Hear our lascivious courtships, see our dalliance,
Taste of the same provoking meats with us,
To ruin of our states! Nay, when our own
Portion is fled, to prey on the remainder,
We call them into fellowship of vice;
Bait 'em with the young chamber-maid, to seal,
And teach 'em all bad ways to buy affliction.
This is one path: but there are millions more,
In which we spoil our own, with leading them.
Well, I thank heaven, I never yet was he
That travell'd with my son, before sixteen,
To shew him the Venetian courtezans;
Nor read the grammar of cheating I had made,
To my sharp boy, at twelve; repeating still
The rule, *Get money; still, get money, boy;*
No matter by what means; money will do
More, boy, than my lord's letter. Neither have I
Drest snails or mushrooms curiously before him,
Perfumed my sauces, and taught him how to make them;
Preceding still, with my gray gluttony,
At all the ord'naries, and only fear'd
His palate should degenerate, not his manners.
These are the trade of fathers now; however,
My son, I hope, hath met within my threshold
None of these household precedents, which are strong,
And swift, to rape youth to their precipice.
But let the house at home be ne'er so clean
Swept, or kept sweet from filth, nay dust and cobwebs,

If he will live abroad with his companions,
In dung and leystals, it is worth a fear;
Nor is the danger of conversing less
Than all that I have mention'd of example.

The Fair Maid of the Exchange

Thomas Heywood
1607

Scene: London

Male—Serio-Comic
   Frank: a young man about town, 20s

   When he suspects that he is falling in love, Frank cannot help waxing rhapsodically
   about the young lady in question.

FRANK: I am not well, and yet I am not ill,
I am, what am I? not in love I hope?
In love? let me examine my selfe, who should I love? who did I last
converse with, with *Phillis*: why should I love *Phillis*? is she faire? faith
so so: her forehead is pretty, somewhat resembling the forehead of the
signe of the maidenhead in, &c. What's her haire? faith two Bandora
wiars, ther's not the simile: is it likely yet that I am in love? What next?
her cheekes they have a reasonable scarlet, never a Diars daughter in
the townes goes beyond her. Well, yet I am not in love. Nay, she hath a
mole in her cheeke too: *Venus* mole was not a more naturall; but what
of that? I am *Adonis*, and will not love. Good *Venus* pardon me, Let us
descend: her chinne, O *Hellen*, *Hellen*, where's your dimple *Hellen*? it
was your dimple that bewitcht *Paris*, and without your dimple I will
not love you *Hellen*, No, yet I am safe. Her hand, lets handle that, I saw
her hand, and it was lilly white, I toucht her palme, and it was soft and
smooth: and then, what then? her hand did then bewitch me, I shall bee
in love now out of hand. In love? shall I that ever yet have prophan'd
love, now fall to worship him? Shall I that have ieasted at lovers sighes
now raise whirle-windes? Shall I that have flowted ay-mees once a
quarter, now practise ay-mees every minute? shall I defie hat-bands,
and tread garters and shoo-strings under my feet? shall I fall to falling
bands and bee a ruffin no longer? I must; I am now liege man to *Cupid*,
and have read all these informations in his booke of statutes, the first
chapter, page *millefimo nono*, therefore, hat-band avaunt, ruffe regard
your selfe, garters adue, shoo-strings so and so; I am a poor enamorate,
and enforc'd with the Poet to say, Love orecomes all, and I that love
obey.

Friar Bacon and Friar Bungay

Robert Greene
1589–92

Scene: Oxford

Male—Serio-Comic
    Friar Bacon: a man obsessed with conjuring, 50–60

> The industrious Friar Bacon has constructed a strange brass head that he hopes will grant him dominion over the forces of evil. Here, the friar instructs his student to watch over the head while he sleeps.

FRIAR BACON: Miles, where were you?

[*MILES:* Here, sir.]

FRIAR BACON: How chance you tarry so long?

[*MILES:* Think you that the watching of the Brazen Head craves no furniture?[205] I warrant you, sir, I have so armed myself that if all your devils come, I will not fear them an inch.]

FRIAR BACON: Miles, thou know's that I have dived into hell,
And sought the darkest palaces of fiends;
That with my magic spells great Belcephon
Hath left his lodge and kneeled at my cell;
The rafters of the earth rent from the poles,
And three-formed Luna[206] hid her silver looks,
Trembling upon her concave continent,
When Bacon read upon his magic book.
With seven years' tossing[207] necromantic charms,
Poring upon dark Hecat's[208] principles,
I have framed out a monstrous head of brass,
That, by the enchanting forces of the devil,
Shall tell out strange and uncouth[209] aphorisms,[210]
And girt fair England with a wall of brass.
Bungay and I have watched these threescore days,

---

[205]apparatus
[206]Selene in heaven, Artemis on earth, Hecate in the lower world.
[207]turning over
[208]Goddess of witchcraft.
[209]unknown
[210]principles

And now our vital spirits crave some rest.
If Argus lived, and had his hundred eyes,
They could not over-watch Phobetor's[211] night.
Now, Miles, in thee rests Friar Bacon's weal:
The honor and renown of all his life
Hangs in the watching of this Brazen Head;
Therefore I charge thee by the immortal God,
That holds the souls of men within his fist,
This night thou watch; for ere the morning-star
Sends out his glorious glister on the north,
The head will speak; then, Miles, upon thy life,
Wake me: for then by magic art I'll work
To end my seven years' task with excellence.
If that a wink but shut thy watchful eye,
Then farewell Bacon's glory and his fame!
Draw close the curtains, Miles: now for thy life,
Be watchful, and—
(*Here he falls asleep.*)

---

[211]Son of Morpheus.

Gammer Gurton's Needle

William Stevenson
1566

Scene: Tudor England

Male—Serio-Comic
> Diccon: a licensed beggar newly released from Bedlam, 30–50

> When the wandering Diccon arrives at the home of Gammer Gurton, he finds all in
> an uproar due to the loss of the lady's sewing needle.

DICCON: Many a mile have I walked, divers and sundry ways,
and many a good man's house have I been at in my days,
Many a gossip's cup in my time have I tasted,
And many a broach[212] and spit have I both turned and basted,
Many a piece of bacon have I had out of their balks[213]
In running over the country with long and weare[214] walks;
Yet came my foot never within those doorcheeks,[215]
To seek flesh, or fish, garlic, onions, or leeks,
That ever I saw a sort[216] in such a plight
As here within this house appeareth to my sight!
There is howling and scowling, all cast in a dump,
With whewling and puling, as though they had lost a trump;[217]
Sighing and sobbing they weep and they wail,
I marvel in my mind what the devil they ail.
The old trot[218] sits groaning, with "alas!" and "alas!"
And Tib wrings her hands, and takes on in worse case.
With poor Cock, their boy, they be driven in such fits
I fear me the folks be not well in their wits.
Ask them what they ail, or who brought them in this stay,[219]
They answer not at all but "alack!" and "welaway!"

212skewer
213Beams, whence the bacon was hung.
214weary(?)
215entrances
216group
217In a card game.
218hag
219plight

When I saw it booted[220] not, out at doors I hied me,
And caught a slip of bacon, when I saw that none spied me,
Which I intend not far hence, unless my purpose fail,
Shall serve for a shoeing-horn[221] to draw on two pots of ale.

---

[220]availed
[221]I.e., a means of achieving.

The Knight of the Burning Pestle

Francis Beaumont
1613

Scene: at the presentation of a play

Male—Serio-Comic
     Ralph: a grocer's assistant turned actor, 20s

   Ralph's employer has written a play and insists that his simple assistant portray the
   title role of the Knight of the Burning Pestle. Here, Ralph hams it up in an elaborate
   and long-winded death scene.

(Enter Ralph, with a forked arrow through his head.)
RALPH: When I was mortal, this my costive corpse
Did lap up figs and raisins in the Strand;
Where sitting, I espi'd a lovely dame,
Whose master wrought with lingel[222] and with awl,
And underground he vamped many a boot.
Straight did her love prick forth me, tender sprig,
To follow feats of arms in warlike wise
Through Waltham Desert; where I did perform
Many achievements, and did lay on ground
Huge Barbaroso, that insulting giant,
And all his captives soon set at liberty.
Then honor prick'd me from my native soil
Into Moldavia, where I gain'd the love
Of Pompiona, his beloved daughter;
But yet prov'd constant to the black thumb'd maid,
Susan, and scorned Pompiona's love.
Yet liberal I was, and gave her pins,
And money for her father's officers.
I then returned home, and thrust myself
In action, and by all men chosen was
Lord of the May, where I did flourish it,
With scarfs and rings, and posy in my hand.
After this action I preferred was,
And chosen city-captain at Mile-End,

[222]Shoemaker's waxed thread.

With hat and feather, and with leading-staff,
And train'd my men, and brought them all off clear,
Save one man that beray'd[223] him with the noise.
But all these things I Ralph did undertake
Only for my beloved Susan's sake.
Then coming home, and sitting in my shop
With apron blue, Death came unto my stall
To cheapen[224] *aqua vitæ*; but ere I
Could take the bottle down and fill a taste,
Death caught a pound of pepper in his hand,
And sprinkled all my face and body o'er,
And in an instant vanished away.
[*CIT:* 'T is a pretty fiction, i' faith.]
RALPH: Then took I up my bow and shaft in hand,
And walk'd into Moorfields to cool myself;
But there grim cruel Death met me again,
And shot this forked arrow through my head;
And now I faint; therefore be warn'd by me,
My fellows every one, of forked heads!
Farewell, all you good boys in merry London!
Ne'er shall we more upon Shrove-Tuesday meet,
And pluck down house of iniquity;——[224A]
My pain increaseth—I shall never more
Hold open, whilst another pumps both legs,
Nor daub a satin gown with rotten eggs;
Set up a stake, oh, never more I shall!
I die! fly, fly, my soul, to Grocers' Hall!
Oh, oh, oh, &c.

---

[223]befouled
[224]Bargain for.
224A On Shrove Tuesday, the apprentices' holiday, they used to band together and loot the brothels.

The Malcontent

John Marston
1604

Scene: Genoa

Male—Dramatic
    Malevole: the Duke of Genoa in disguise, 30–40

When his power is usurped, the duke disguises himself as the dire Malevole, which allows him to roam freely in the court. Here, he takes a moment to council a foolish vassal, who intends to leave his young wife at court while he travels abroad.

MALEVOLE: Embassador! Now, for thy country's honour, preethee do not put up mutton and porridge in thy clock-bag:[225] thy young lady wife goes to Florence with thee too, does she not?
[*BILIOSO:* No, I leave her at the palace.]
MALEVOLE: At the palace? now discretion shield,[226] man! for God's love let's ha' no more cuckolds, Hymen begins to put off his saffron robe.[227] Keep thy wife i' the state of grace. Heart o' truth, I would sooner leave my lady singled in a bordello[228] than in the Genoa palace.

Sin there appearing in her sluttish shape

Would soon grow loathsome, even to blushes' sense,

Surfeit would cloak intemperate appetite,

Make the soul scent the rotten breath of lust:

When in an Italian lascivious palace,

A lady guardianless,

Left to the push of all allurement,

The strong'st incitements to immodesty,

To have her bound, incens'd[229] with wanton sweets,

Her veins fill'd high with heating[230] delicates,

Soft rest, sweet music, amorous masquerers,

Lascivious banquets, sin it self gilt o'er,

Strong fantasy tricking up strange delights,

----

[225]valise
[226]forbid
[227]Customarily worn by Hymen in a masque.
[228]brothel (Ital.)
[229]Excited, playing on the sense of perfumed.
[230]I.e., exciting the blood

Presenting it dressed pleasingly to sense,
Sense leading it unto the soul, confirm'd
With potent example, impudent custom,
Enticed by that great bawd opportunity—
Thus being prepar'd, clap to her easy ear
Youth in good clothes, well-shap'd, rich, fair-spoken, promising-
noble,[231] ardent blood-full, witty, flattering: Ulysses absent, O Ithaca,
can chastest Penelope hold out?

[231]Heir to noble rank.

Michaelmas Term

Thomas Middleton
1605

Scene: London

#1 Male—Serio-Comic
      Andrew Lethe: an upstart adventurer, 20s

    Here, a scheming young man plots to wed the daughter of a wealthy merchant
    while simultaneously seducing the girl's mother.

ANDREW LETHE: [Easily remember'd that, you know!]
(*Exeunt all but LETHE.*)
But now unto my present business. The daughter yields, and Quomodo
consents, only my Mistress Quomodo, her mother, without regard runs
full against[232] me, and sticks[233] hard. Is there no law for a woman that
will run upon a man at her own apperil?[234] Why should not she
consent, knowing my state, my sudden fortunes? I can command[235] a
custard, and other bake-meats, death of sturgeon;[236] I could keep house
with nothing. What friends have I! How well am I beloved, e'en quite
throughout the scullery![237] Not consent? 'Tis e'en as I have writ; I'll be
hang'd and she[238] love me not herself, and would rather preserve me as
a private friend to her own pleasures, than any way advance her
daughter upon me to beguile herself. Then how have I relieved her in
that point? Let me peruse this letter.

    (*Reading.*) "Good Mistress Quomodo, or rather, as I hope ere the
Term end, Mother Quomodo, since only your consent keeps aloof
off,[239] and hinders the copulation of your daughter, what may I think,
but that it is a mere[240] affection in you, doting upon some small inferior
virtue of mine, to draw me in upon yourself? If the case stand so, I have
comfort for you; for this you may well assure yourself, that by the

---

[232]Absolutely opposes.
[233]persists
[234]peril (Dyce)
[235]Get for the asking.
[236]Perhaps an oath (Bullen), or a keg of sturgeon (Sampson); the text may be corrupt.
[237]Kitchen, presumably at Court (Eccles).
[238]if she
[239]Remains withheld.
[240]sheer (Price).

marriage of your daughter I have the better means and opportunity to yourself, and without the least suspicion."

This is moving stuff, and that works best with a citizen's wife. But who shall I get to convey this now? My page I ha' lent forth; my pander I have employ'd about the country to look out[241] some third sister,[242] or entice some discontented gentlewoman from her husband, whom the laying out[243] of my appetite shall maintain. Nay, I'll deal like an honorable gentleman, I'll be kind to women; that which I gather i'th' day, I'll put into their purses at night. You shall have no cause to rail at me; no, faith, I'll keep you in good fashion, ladies; no meaner men than knights shall ransom home[244] your gowns and recover your smocks;[245] I'll not dally with you.

Some poor widow woman would come as a necessary bawd now; and see where fitly comes—

#2 Male—Serio-Comic
 Hellgill: a pander, 20–30

 Hellgill here does his best to convince a country wench to provide amorous services for his master.

HELLGILL: Come, leave your puling[246] and sighing.
[*COUNTRY WENCH:* Beshrew you now, why did you entice me from my father?]
HELLGILL: Why? To thy better advancement. Wouldst thou, a pretty, beautiful, juicy squall,[247] live in a poor thrum'd[248] house i'th' country in such servile habiliments,[249] and may well pass for a gentlewoman i'th' city? Does not five hundred do so, think'st thou, and with worse faces? Oh, now in these latter days, the devil reigning, 'tis an age for cloven[250] creatures. But why sad now? Yet indeed 'tis the fashion of

---

[241]Look out for, seek out.
[242]Since daughters were often married off by seniority, a girl with two older unwed sisters might well despair of ever marrying (especially if, as Price suggests, the family cannot afford three dowries), and so be susceptible.
[243]Exercising, expenditure.
[244]From pawn (Sampson).
[245]Women's undergarments.
[246]whining
[247]Young minx (Cotgrave's *Dictionary of the French and English Tongues* [1611], s.v., "Obereau," cited in Bullen).
[248]thatched (Dyce)
[249]apparel
[250]Devilish (since he had cloven hoofs).

any courtesan to be seasick i'th' first voyage, but at next she proclaims open wars, like a beaten[251] soldier. Why, Northamptonshire[252] lass, dost dream of virginity now? Remember a loose-bodied[253] gown, wench, and let it go; wires and tires, bents and bums, felts and falls,[254] thou shalt deceive the world, that gentlewomen indeed shall not be known from others. I have a master to whom I must prefer[255] thee after the aforesaid decking,[256] Lethe by name, a man of one most admired property:[257] he can both love thee, and for thy better advancement be thy pander himself, an exc'llent spark of humility.[258]

#3 Male—Dramatic
Father: a man searching for his daughter, 40–50

When his daughter runs away from home to become the mistress of the rougish Andrew Lithe, her father resolves to find her.

FATHER: Where shall I seek her now? Oh, if she knew
The dangers that attend on women's lives,
She would rather lodge under a poor thatch'd roof
Than under carved ceilings.[259] She was my joy,
And all content that I receiv'd from life,
My dear and only daughter.
What says the note she left? Let me again
With staider grief peruse it.
(*Reading.*) "Father, wonder not at my so sudden departure, without
your leave or knowledge. Thus, under pardon, I excuse it: had you had
knowledge of it, I know you would have sought to restrain it, and
hinder me from what I have long desir'd. Being now happily
prefer'd[260] to a gentleman's service in London, about Holborn,[261] if you
please to send, you may hear well of me."

[251]experienced (Price)

[252]Rural county in central England.

[253]Suggests moral "looseness" (see l. 25); cf. Middleton's *The Family of Love*, V.iii.192–193: "a crew of narrow-ruffed, strait-laced yet loose-bodied dames."

[254]*Wires* were frames for the hair or ruff; *tires*, headdresses; *bents*, frames to extend dresses at the hips; *bums*, padding about the waist; *felts*, hats; *falls*, collars.

[255]Recommend, promote, advance.

[256]Dressing up.

[257]Attribute, quality.

[258]Since he will share her (Eccles).

[259]In the homes of the wealthy.

[260]See note.

[261]District with a poor reputation (Sugden).

As false as she is disobedient!
I've made larger inquiry, left no place,
Where gentry keeps,[262] unsought,[263] yet cannot hear,[264]
Which drives me most into a shareful fear.
Woe worth[265] th'infected cause that makes me visit
This man-devouring city, where I spent
My unshapen[266] youth, to be my age's curse,
And surfeited away my name and state[267]
In swinish riots, that now, being sober,
I do awake a beggar. I may hate her.
Whose youth voids[268] wine, his age is curs'd with water.
Oh heavens, I know the price of ill too sell,
What the confusions are, in whom they dwell,
And how soon maids are to their ruins won;
One minute, and eternally undone;
So in mine may it, may it not be thus!
Though she be poor, her honor's precious.
May be my present form, and her fond[269] fear,
May chase her from me, if her eye should get me;
And therefore, as my love and wants advise,
I'll serve,[270] until I find her, in disguise.
Such is my care to fright her from base evils,
I leave calm state to live amongst you, devils.

---

[262]Dwells (Dyce), frequents.
[263]unsearched
[264]News of her.
[265]Woe be unto (Sampson).
[266]Unformed, undisciplined.
[267]Good name and estate, inheritance.
[268]Wastes (Price) or vomits.
[269]foolish
[270]Become a servant.

Much Ado About Nothing
William Shakespeare
1598

Scene: Messina

Male—Serio-Comic
    Benedick: a young lord of Padua, 20s

   When Benedick's friend, Claudio falls in love, Benedick contemplates the strange
   changes that love can make in the heart of a man.

BENEDICK: I do much wonder that one man, seeing how much
another man is a fool when he dedicates his behaviours to love, will,
after he hath laughed at such shallow follies in others, become the argument of his own scorn by falling in love: and such a man is Claudio. I
have known when there was no music with him but the drum and the
fife; and now had he rather hear the tabor and the pipe: I have known
when he would have walked ten mile a-foot to see a good armour; and
now will he lie ten nights awake, carving the fashion of a new doublet.
He was wont to speak plain and to the purpose, like an honest man and
a soldier; and now is he turned orthography; his words are a very
fantastical banquet, just so many strange dishes. May I be so converted
and see with these eyes? I cannot tell; I think not: I will not be sworn
but love may transform me to an oyster; but I'll take my oath on it, till
he have made an oyster of me, he shall never make me such a fool. One
woman is fair, yet I am well; another is wise, yet I am well; another
virtuous, yet I am well; but till all graces be in one woman, one woman
shall not come in my grace. Rich she shall be, that's certain; wise, or I'll
none; virtuous, or I'll never cheapen her; fair, or I'll never look on her;
mild, or come not near me; noble, or not I for an angel; of good
discourse, an excellent musician, and her hair shall be of what colour it
please God.

The Revengers' Tragedy

Cyril Tourneur

1607

Scene: A ducal court

Male—Dramatic
Vindice: a man seeking revenge for the murder of the woman he loves, 20–30

> When Vindice's mistress refused the Duke's advances, the enraged nobleman poisoned her. Here, the grieving Vindice roams the castle with her skull, speaking to it as if she were still alive.

VINDICE: Madam his Grace will not be absent long.
Secret? ne'er doubt us Madam; 'twill be worth
Three velvet gowns to your Ladyship;—known?
Few ladies respect that;—disgrace? a poor thin shell,
'Tis the best grace you have to do it well.
I'll save your hand that labour, I'll unmask you.
[*HIPPOLITO:* Why brother, brother.]
VINDICE: Art thou beguil'd now? tut, a lady can,
At such all hid,[271] beguile a wiser man.
Have I not fitted the old surfeiter
With a quaint piece of beaty? Age and bare bone
Are e'er allied in action; here's an eye,
Able to tempt a greatman—to serve God,
A pretty hanging lip, that has forgot now to dissemble:
Methinks this mouth should make a swearer tremble,
A drunkard clasp his teeth, and not undo 'em
To suffer wet damnation to run through 'em.
Here's a cheek keeps her colour, let the wind go whistle;
Spout rain, we fear thee not, be hot or cold,
All's one with us; and is not he absurd,
Whose fortunes are upon their faces set,
That fear no other God but wind and wet?
[*HIPPOLITO:* Brother y'ave spoke that right;
Is this the form that living shone so bright?]
VINDICE: The very same,—

....

[271]At such a game of hide and seek.

And now methinks I could e'en chide myself,
For doating on her beauty, tho' her death
Shall be reveng'd after no common action;
Does the silk-worm expend her yellow labours
For thee? for thee does she undo herself?
Are lordships[272] sold to maintain ladyships[273]
For the poor benefit of a bewitching minute?
Why does yon fellow falsify high-ways[274]
And put his life between the judge's lips,
To refine such a thing, keeps horse and men
To beat their valours[275] for her?
Surely, we're all mad people, and they
Whom we think are, are not,—we mistake those,
'Tis we are mad in sense, they but in clothes.
[*HIPPOLITO:* Faith and in clothes too we, give us our due.[276]]
VINDICE: Does every proud and self-affecting dame
Camphire[277] her face for this? and grieve her Maker
In sinful baths of milk,—when many an infant starves,
For her superfluous outside, all for this?
Who now bids twenty pound a night, prepares
Music, perfumes, and sweetmeats? all are husht,
Thou may'st lie chaste now! It were fine methinks,
To have thee seen at revels, forgetful feasts,
And unclean brothels; sure 'twould fright the sinner
And make him a good coward, put a reveller
Out of his antic amble
And cloy an epicure with empty dishes.
Here might a scornful and ambitious woman
Look through and through herself;—see ladies, with false forms
You deceive men, but cannot deceive worms.
Now to my tragic business,—look you brother,
I have not fashion'd this only for show

---

[272]estates
[273]I.e., in fine clothes and adornments.
[274]Turn highwayman.
[275]Use up their strengths.
[276]Alluding to the disguise Vindice wears.
[277]Camphor (used as a perfume in soaps and cosmetics).

And useless property,[278] no, it shall bear a part
E'en in its own revenge. This very skull,
Whose mistress the Duke poisoned, with this drug
The mortal curse of the earth, shall be reveng'd
In the like strain, and kiss his lips to death;
As much as the dumb thing can, he shall feel:
What fails in poison, we'll supply in steel.

---

[278]I.e., stage property.

The Spanish Tragedy

Thomas Kyd
1584–89

Scene: Spain

#1 Male—Dramatic
 Ghost of Andrea: an unhappy spirit, 20–30

> Here, the ghost of a soldier slain in the recent war with Portugal wanders the corridors of the royal castle while lamenting his fate.

GHOST: When this eternal substance of my soul
Did live imprisoned in my wanton flesh,
Each in their function serving other's need,
I was a courtier in the Spanish Court.
My name was Don Andrea; my descent,
Though not ignoble, yet inferior far
To gracious fortunes of my tender youth:
For there in prime and pride of all my years,
By duteous service and deserving love,
In secret I possessed a worthy dame,
Which hight[279] sweet Bel-imperia by name.
but in the harvest of my summer joys
Death's winter nipped the blossoms of my bliss,
Forcing divorce betwixt my love and me.
For in the late conflict with Portingale[280]
My valor drew me into danger's mouth
Till life to death made passage through my wounds.
When I was slain, my soul descended straight[281]
To pass the flowing stream of Acheron;[282]
But churlish Charon,[283] only boatman there,
Said that, my rites of burial not performed,
I might not sit amongst his passengers.

---

[279]was called
[280]Portugal
[281]This and the following 67 lines give a description of the underworld based on Virgil's *Aeneid*, Book VI.
[282]River in Hell.
[283]Ferryman in Hell.

Ere Sol had slept three nights in Thetis' lap,[284]
And slaked his smoking chariot in her flood,
By Don Horatio, our Knight Marshal's son,
My funerals and obsequies were done.
Then was the ferryman of hell content
To pass me over to the slimy strand
That leads to fell Avernus'[285] ugly waves.
There, pleasing Cerberus[286] with honeyed speech,
I passed the perils of the foremost porch.
Not far from hence, amidst ten thousand souls,
Sat Minos, Aeacus, and Rhadamanth,[287]
To whom no sooner gan I make approach,
To crave a passport for my wand'ring ghost,
But Minos, in graven leaves of lottery,[288]
Drew forth the manner of my life and death.
"This knight," quoth he, "both lived and died in love,
And for his love tried fortune of the wars,
And by war's fortune lost both love and live."
"Why then," said Aeacus, "convey him hence
To walk with lovers in our fields of love,
And spend the course of everlasting time
Under green myrtle trees and cypress shades."
"No, no," said Rhadamanth, "it were not well
With loving souls to place a martialist,[289]
He died in war and must to martial fields,
Where wounded Hector lives in lasting pain,
And Achilles' Myrmidons[290] do scour the plain."
Then Minos, mildest censor[291] of the three,
Made this device[292] to end the difference:
"Send him," quoth he, "to our infernal King,

---

[284]Sea goddess.
[285]Lake in Hell.
[286]Hell guard.
[287]Judges in Hell.
[288]The lottery slip on which was engraved the record of Andrea's life.
[289]soldier
[290]Achilles' followers.
[291]judge
[292]plan

To doom[293] him as best seems his majesty."
To this effect my passport straight was drawn.
In keeping on my way to Pluto's[294] Court,
Through dreadful shades of ever-glooming night,
I saw more sights than thousand tongues can tell,
Or pens can write, or mortal hearts can think.
Three ways there were: that on the right-hand side
Was ready way unto the 'foresaid fields
Where lovers live and bloody martialists,
But either[295] sort[296] contained within his bounds.
The left-hand path, declining fearfully,
Was ready downfall to the deepest hell,[297]
Where bloody Furies shake their whips of steel,
And poor Ixion[298] turns an endless wheel;
Where usurers are choked with melting gold,
And wantons[299] are embraced with ugly snakes,
And murders groan with never-killing wounds,
And perjured wights[300] scalded in boiling lead,
And all foul sins with torments overwhelmed.
'Twixt these two ways I trod the middle path,
Which brought me to the fair Elysian green,[301]
In midst whereof there stands a stately tower,
The walls of brass, the gates of adamant.
Here finding Pluto with his Proserpine,[302]
I showed my passport, humbled on my knee;
Whereat fair Proserpine began to smile,
And begged that only she might give my doom.[303]
Pluto was pleased and sealed it with a kiss.

....

[293]judge
[294]God of the underworld.
[295]each
[296]group
[297]Tartarus
[298]Punished by Zeus.
[299]Licentious individuals.
[300]persons
[301]Elysium
[302]Goddess of Hell.
[303]sentence

Forthwith, Revenge, she rounded[304] thee in th'ear,
And bade thee lead me through the gates of Horn[305]
Where dreams have passage in the silent night.
No sooner had she spoke but we were here,
I wot[306] not how, in twinkling of an eye.

#2 Male—Dramatic
    Hieronimo: the Marshal of Spain, 40–50

Hieronimo's son, Horatio, has been murdered by the Prince of Portugal with his accomplices. Here, the Marshal discovers his son's body, which has been hung by the murderers in an arbor.

HIERONIMO: What outcries pluck me from my naked bed,
And chill my throbbing heart with trembling fear,
Which never danger yet could daunt before?
Who calls Hieronimo? speak, here I am.
I did not slumber, therefore 'twas no dream.
No, no, it was some woman cried for help,
And here within this garden did she cry,
And in this garden must I rescue her.
But stay, what murd'rous spectacle is this?
A man hanged up and all the murderers gone,
And in my bower, to lay the guilt on me.
This place was made for pleasure, not for death.
(*He cuts the body down.*)
Those garments that he wears I oft have seen—
Alas, it is Horatio, my sweet son!
O no, but he that whilom[307] was my son!
O was it thou that call'dst me from my bed?
O speak, if any spark of life remain!
I am thy father. Who hath slain my son?
What savage monster, not of human kind,
Hath here been glutted with thy harmless blood,
And left thy bloody corpse dishonored here,
For me, amidst these dark and deathful shades,

[304]whispered
[305]gates of sleep
[306]know
[307]formerly

To drown thee with an ocean of my tears?
O heavens, why made you night to cover sin?
By day this deed of darkness had not been.
O earth, why didst thou not in time devour
The vild[308] profaner of this sacred bower?
O poor Horatio, what hadst thou misdone,
To lose thy life ere life was new begun?
O wicked butcher, whatsoe'er thou wert,
How could thou strangle virtue and desert?
Ay me most wretched, that have lost my joy,
In losing my Horatio, my sweet boy!

---

[308]vile

Such Stuff as Dreams Are Made of

Calderon de la Barca
@ 1630

Scene: the Polish frontier

Male—Dramatic
> Segismund: captive prince of Poland

> Imprisoned in a desolate fortress and held by a large and heavy chain, Segismund here vents his spleen to the night sky.

SEGISMUND: Once more the storm has roar'd itself away,
Splitting the crags of God as it retires;
But sparing still what it should only blast,
This guilty piece of human handiwork,
And all that are within it. Oh, how oft,
How oft, within or her abroad, have I
Waited, and in the whisper of my heart
Pray'd for the slanting hand of heaven to strike
The blow myself I dared not, out of fear
Of that Hereafter, worse, they say, than here,
Plunged headlong in, but, till dismissal waited,
To wipe at last all sorrow from men's eyes,
And make this heavy dispensation clear.
Thus have I borne till now, and still endure,
Crouching in sullen impotence day by day,
Till some such out-burst of the elements
Like this rouses the sleeping fire within;
And standing thus upon the threshold of
Another night about to close the door
Upon one wretched day to open it
On one yet wretcheder because one more;—
Once more, you savage heavens, I ask of you—
I, looking up to those relentless eyes
That, now the greater lamp is gone below,
Begin to muster in the listening skies;
In all the shining circuits you have gone

About this theatre of human woe,
What greater sorrow have you gazed upon
Than down this narrow chink you witness still;
And which, did you yourselves not fore-devise,
You register'd for others to fulfil!
[*FIFE:* This is some Laureate at a birth-day ode;
No wonder we went rhyming.]
[*ROS:* Hush! And now
See, starting to his feet, he strides about
Far as his tether'd steps—]
SEGISMUND: And if the chain
You help'd to rivet round me did contract
Since guiltless infancy from guilt in act;
Of what in aspiration or in thought
Guilty, but in resentment of the wrong
That wreaks revenge on wrong I never wrought
By excommunication from the free
Inheritance that all created life,
Beside myself, is born to—from the wings
That range your own immeasurable blue,
Down to the poor, mute, scale-imprison'd things,
That yet are free to wander, glide, and pass
About that under-sapphire, whereinto
Yourselves transfusing you yourselves englass!
[*ROS:* What mystery is this?]
[*FIFE:* Why, the man's mad:
That's all the mystery. That's why he's chain'd—
And why—]
SEGISMUND: Nor Nature's guiltless life alone—
But that which lives on blood and rapine; nay,
Charter'd with larger liberty to slay
Their guiltless kind, the tyrants of the air
Soar zenith-upward with their screaming prey,
Making pure heaven drop blood upon the stage
Of under earth, where lion, wolf, and bear,
And they that on their treacherous velvet wear

Figure and constellation like your own,[309]
With their still living slaughter bound away
Over the barriers of the mountain cage,
Against which one, blood-guiltless, and endued
With aspiration and with aptitude
Transcending other creatures, day by day
Beats himself mad with unavailing rage!
[*FIFE:* Why, that must be the meaning of my mule's
Rebellion—]
[*ROS:* Hush!]
SEGISMUND: But then if murder be
The law by which not only conscience-blind
Creatures, but man too prospers with his kind;
Who leaving all his guilty fellows free,
Under your fatal auspice and divine
Compulsion, leagued in some mysterious ban
Against one innocent and helpless man,
Abuse their liberty to murder mine:
And sworn to silence, like their masters mute
In heaven, and like them twiring through the mask
Of darkness, answering to all I ask,
Point up to them whose work they execute!

---

[309]"Some report that they"—(panthers)—"have one marke on the shoulders resembling the moone, growing and decreasing as she doth, sometimes showing a full compasse, and otherwhiles hollowed and pointed with tips like the hornes." —*Philemon Holland's Pliny*, b. viii. c. 17.

Tamburlaine the Great

Christopher Marlowe
1590

Scene: Damascus

Male—Dramatic
   Tamburlaine: a Scythian shepherd turned blood-thirsty conqueror, 30s

   Here, Tamburlaine persuades Techelles, a captain of the Persian army, to join with
   him in his war against the king.

TAMBURLAINE: Noble and mild this Persian seems to be,
If outward habit judge the inward man.
[*TECHELLES:* His deep affections make him passionate.]
TAMBURLAINE: With what a majesty he rears his looks!
In thee, thou valiant man of Persia,
I see the folly of thy emperor.
Art thou but captain of a thousand horse,
That by charácters graven in thy brows,
And by thy martial face and stout aspect,
Deserv'st to have the leading of an host!
Forsake thy king, and do but join with me,
And we will triumph over all the world.
I hold the Fates bound fast in iron chains,
And with my hand turn Fortune's wheel about:
And sooner shall the sun fall from his sphere
Than Tamburlaine be slain or overcome.
Draw forth thy sword, thou mighty man-at-arms,
Intending but to raze[310] my charmed skin,
And Jove himself will stretch his hand from heaven
To ward the blow and shield me safe from harm.
See how he rains down heaps of gold in showers,
As if he meant to give my soldiers pay!
And as a sure and grounded argument,
That I shall be the monarch of the East,
He sends this Soldan's daughter, rich and brave,

---

[310]Graze, scratch.

To be my Queen and portly[311] Emperess.[312]
If thou wilt stay with me, renowned man,
And lead thy thousand horse with my conduct,[313]
Besides thy share of this Egyptian prize,
Those thousand horse shall sweat with martial spoil
Of conquer'd kingdoms and of cities sack'd.
Both we will walk upon the lofty clifts,[314]
And Christian merchants that with Russian stems[315]
Plough up huge furrows in the Caspian sea,
Shall vail[316] to us, as lords of all the lake.
Both we will reign as consuls of the earth,
And mighty kings shall be our senators.
Jove sometime masked in a shepherd's weed,
And by those steps that he hath scal'd the Heavens
May we become immortal like the gods.
Join with me now in this my mean estate,
(I call it mean because, being yet obscure,
The nations far remov'd admire me not,)
And when my name and honour shall be spread
As far as Boreas[317] claps his brazen wings,
Or fair Boötes[318] sends his cheerful light,
Then shalt thou be competitor with me,
And sit with Tamburlaine in all his majesty.

---

[311]stately
[312]Marlowe's meter often demands the addition of a syllable in such words.
[313]Under my direction.
[314]cliffs
[315]ships
[316]salute
[317]North wind.
[318]A northern constellation.

The Tempest

William Shakespeare
1611

Scene: an enchanted island

Male—Dramatic
 Prospero: exiled duke turned magician, 50–60

 When his dukedom is restored to him, Prospero renounces his magic.

PROSPERO: Ye elves of hills, brooks, standing lakes and groves,
And ye that on the sands with printless foot
Do chase the ebbing Neptune and do fly him
When he comes back; you demi-puppets that
By moonshine do the green sour ringlets make,
Whereof the ewe not bites, and you whose pastime
Is to make midnight mushrooms, that rejoice
To hear the solemn curfew; by whose aid,
Weak masters though ye be, I have bedimm'd
The noontide sun, call'd forth the mutinous winds,
And 'twixt the green sea and the azured vault
Set roaring war: to the dread rattling thunder
Have I given fire and rifted Jove's stout oak
With his own bolt; the strong-based promontory
Have I made shake and by the spurs pluck'd up
The pine and cedar: graves at my command
Have waked their sleepers, oped, and let 'em forth
By my so potent art. But this rough magic
I here abjure, and, when I have required
Some heavenly music, which even now I do,
To work mine end upon their senses that
This airy charm is for, I'll break my staff,
Bury it certain fathoms in the earth,
And deeper than did ever plummet sound
I'll drown my book.

Three Judgments at a Blow

Calderon de la Barca
@ 1630

Scene: the court of Arragon

Male—Dramatic
   Don Lope de Urrea: a man pleading for the life of his son, 50–60

   Don Urrea's son has been condemned for killing another man in a duel. Here, Don
   Urrea pleads his son's innocence to the king in hopes of extracting a royal pardon.

DON LOPE DE URREA: So please your Majesty, listen to one,
Of whom already you have largely heard—
Don Lope de Urrea.
[*KING:* Oh! Don Lope!]
DON LOPE DE URREA: I come not hither to repeat in words
The purport of so many past petitions,
My sorrows now put on a better face
Before your Highness' presence. I beseech you
To hear me patiently.
[*KING:* Speak, Urrea, speak!]
DON LOPE DE URREA: Speak if I can, whose sorrow rising still
Clouds its own utterance. My liege, my son,
Don Lope, loved a lady here; seduced her
By no feign'd vows of marriage, but compell'd
By me, who would not listen to a suit
Without my leave contracted, put it off
From day to day, until the lady, tired
Of a delay that argued treachery,
Engaged her brother in the quarrel; who
With two companions set upon my son
One night to murder him. The lad, whose metal
Would never brook affront, nor cared for odds,
Drew on all three; slew one—a homicide
That nature's common law of self-defence
Permits. The others fled, and set on him
The officers of justice, one of whom
In his escape he struck—

A self-defence against your laws I own
Not so to be excused—then fled himself
Up to the mountains. I must needs confess
He better had deserved an after-pardon
By lawful service in your camp abroad
Than aggravating old offence at home,
By lawless plunder; but your Highness knows
It is an ancient law of honour here
In Arragon, that none of noble blood
In mortal quarrel quit his native ground.
But to return. The woman, twice aggrieved,
Her honour and her brother lost at once,
(For him it was my son slew of the three,)
Now seeks to bring her sorrows into port:
And pitying my grey hairs and misery,
Consents to acquit my son on either count,
Providing I supply her wherewithal
To hide her shame within some holy house;
Which, straiten'd as I am, (that, by my troth,
I scarce, my liege, can find my daily bread,)
I have engaged to do; not only this,
But, in addition to the sum in hand,
A yearly income—which to do, I now
Am crept into my house's poorest rooms,
And, (to such straits may come nobility!)
Have let for hire what should become my rank
And dignity to an old friend, Don Mendo
Torellas, who I hear returns to-day
To Saragossa. It remains, my liege,
That, being by the plaintiff's self absolved,
My son your royal pardon only needs;
Which if not he nor I merit ourselves,
Yet let the merits of a long ancestry,
Who swell your glorious annals with their names
Writ in their blood, plead for us not in vain;
Pity the snows of age that misery
Now thaws in torrents from my eyes; yet more,

Pity a noble lady—my wife—his mother—
Who sits bow'd down with sorrow and disgrace
In her starved house.

Timon of Athens

William Shakespeare
1607

Scene: a cave near Athens

Male—Dramatic
Timon: a misanthrope living in self-imposed exile, 30–50

> When his friends desert him during a time of financial distress, Timon takes his leave of Athenian society and makes a new home in a desolate cave, where he intends to live out his days. Here, Timon curses the shallow nature of humankind as he digs in the earth for roots.

TIMON: O blessed breeding sun, draw from the earth
Rotten humidity; below thy sister's orb
Infect the air! Twinn'd brothers of one womb,
Whose procreation, residence, and birth,
Scarce is dividant, touch them with several fortunes;
The greater scorns the lesser: not nature,
To whom all sores lay siege, can bear great fortunes;
But thy contempt of nature.
Raise me this beggar, and deny't that lord;
The senator shall bear contempt hereditary,
The beggar native honour.
It is the pasture lards the rother's sides,
The want that makes him lean. Who dares, who dares,
In purity of manhood stand upright,
And say "This man's a flatterer"? if one be,
So are they all; for every grise of fortune
Is smooth'd by that below: the learned pate
Ducks to the golden fool: all is oblique;
There's nothing level in our cursed natures,
But direct villany. Therefore, be abhorr'd
All feasts, societies, and throngs of men!
His semblable, yea, himself, Timon disdains:
Destruction fang mankind! Earth, yield me roots! (*Digging.*)
Who seeks for better of thee, sauce his palate
With thy most operant poison! What is here?
Gold? yellow, glittering, precious gold? No, gods,

I am no idle votarist: roots, you clear heavens!
Thus much of this will make black white, foul fair,
Wrong right, base noble, old young, coward valiant.
Ha, you gods! why this? what this, you gods? Why, this
Will lug your priests and servants from your sides,
Pluck stout men's pillows from below their heads:
This yellow slave
Will knit and break religions, bless the accursed,
Make the hoar leprosy adored, place thieves
And give them title, knee and approbation
With senators on the bench: this is it
That makes the wappen'd widow wed again;
She, whom the spital-house and ulcerous sores
Would cast the gorge at, this embalms and spices
To the April day again. Come, damned earth,
Thou common whore of mankind, that put'st odds
Among the rout of nations, I will make thee
Do thy right nature. (*March afar off.*) Ha! a drum? Thou'rt quick,
But yet I'll bury thee: thou'lt go, strong thief,
When gouty keepers of thee cannot stand.
Nay, stay thou out for earnest.

'Tis Pity She's a Whore

John Ford
1627

Scene: Italy

Male—Dramatic
> Giovanni: a tragic young man, 20s

> Here, Giovanni confesses his forbidden passion for his sister, Annabella

GIOVANNI: Lost, I am lost: my fates have doom'd my death.
The more I strive, I love; the more I love,
The less I hope: I see my ruin certain.
What judgment or endeavors could apply
To my incurable and restless wounds
I throughly[319] have examin'd, but in vain:
O that it were not in religion sin
To make our love a god and worship it!
I have even wearied heaven with prayers, dried up
The spring of my continual tears, even starv'd
My veins with daily fasts: what wit or art
Could counsel, I have practic'd; but alas,
I find all these but dreams and old men's tales
To fright unsteady youth; I'm still the same.
Or I must speak, or burst; 'tis not, I know,
My lust, but 'tis my fate that leads me on.
Keep[320] fear and low faint-hearted shame with slaves;
I'll tell her that I love her, though my heart
Were rated at the price of that attempt.
O me! She comes.

---

[319]thoroughly
[320]Live, dwell.

The Tragedy of King Richard II
William Shakespeare
1595

Scene: a castle on the shore of Wales

#1 Male—Dramatic
> Richard II: King of England, 30s

>> When Richard returns to England from his war with Ireland, he discovers that the lords of the realm have risen in revolt. Here, Richard greets his native soil.

KING RICHARD: Needs must I like it well: I weep for joy
To stand upon my kingdom once again.
Dear earth, I do salute thee with my hand,
Though rebels wound thee with their horses' hoofs:
As a long-parted mother with her child
Plays fondly with her tears and smiles in meeting.
So, weeping, smiling, greet I thee, my earth,
And do thee favours with my royal hands.
Feed not thy sovereign's foe, my gentle earth,
Nor with thy sweets comfort his ravenous sense;
But let thy spiders, that suck up thy venom,
And heavy-gaited toads lie in their way,
Doing annoyance to the treacherous feet
Which with usurping steps do trample thee:
Yield stinging nettles to mine enemies;
And when they from thy bosom pluck a flower
Guard it, I pray three, with a lurking adder
Whose double tongue may with a mortal touch
Throw death upon thy sovereign's enemies.
Mock not my senseless conjuration, lords:
This earth shall have a feeling and these stones
Prove armed soldiers, ere her native king
Shall falter under foul rebellion's arms.

#2 Male—Dramatic
> Richard II

>> When the severity of the revolt is revealed to the King, he reminds his followers that no one is ever very far from the grave and that kings are just as ruled by death as any man.

KING RICHARD: No matter where; of comfort no man speak:
Let's talk of graves, of worms and epitaphs;
Make dust our paper and with rainy eyes
Write sorrow on the bosom of the earth,
Let's choose executors and talk of wills:
And yet not so, for what can we bequeath
Save our deposed bodies to the ground?
Our lands, our lives and all are Bolingbroke's,
And nothing can we call our own but death
And that small model of the barren earth
Which serves as paste and cover to our bones.
For God's sake, let us sit upon the ground
And tell sad stories of the death of kings:
How some have been deposed; some slain in war;
Some haunted by the ghosts they have deposed;
Some poison'd by their wives; some sleeping kill'd;
All murder'd: for within the hollow crown
That rounds the mortal temples of a king
Keeps Death his court and there the antic sits,
Scoffing his state and grinning at his pomp,
Allowing him a breath, a little scene,
To monarchize, be fear'd and kill with looks,
Infusing him with self and vain conceit,
As if this flesh which walls about our life
Were brass impregnable, and humour'd thus
Comes at the last and with a little pin
Bores through his castle wall, and farewell king!
Cover your heads and mock not flesh and blood
With solemn reverence: throw away respect,
Tradition, form and ceremonious duty,
For you have but mistook me all this while:
I live with bread like you, feel want,
Taste grief, need friends: subjected thus,
How can you say to me, I am a king?

The Two Noble Kinsmen

John Fletcher and William Shakespeare
1634

Scene: Athens

#1 Male—Dramatic
   Arcite: a knight of Thebes, 20s

> Arcite has recently escaped the royal prison in Athens. Here, he takes a moment to ponder his love for Emilia, a noblewoman of Athens. His thoughts then turn to Palamon, his cousin, who is still imprisoned in Athens.

ARCITE: The duke has lost Hippolyta; each took
A several[321] land.[322] This is a solemn rite
They owe bloom'd May, and the Athenians pay it
To th' heart of ceremony. O Queen Emilia,
Fresher than May, sweeter
Than her gold buttons[323] on the boughs, or all
Th'enamell'd[324] knacks[325] o'th' mead or garden, yea
We challenge too the bank of any nymph[326]
That makes the stream seem flowers; thou, O jewel
O'th' wood, o'th' world, hast likewise blest a pace[327]
With thy sole presence. In thy rumination
That I, poor man, might eftsoons[328] come between
And chop on[329] some cold[330] thought! Thrice blessed chance
To drop on such a mistress, expectation
Most guiltless on't.[331] Tell me, O Lady Fortune,
Next after Emily my sovereign, how far
I may be proud. She takes strong note of me,
Hath made me near her, and this beauteous morn,

---

[321]different
[322]Glade; clearing.
[323]buds
[324]Variously colored.
[325]Ornaments; i.e., flowers.
[326]Water spirit, here "river."
[327]Passage through woods.
[328]immediately
[329]interrupt
[330]chaste
[331]Without premeditation of it.

The prim'st[332] of all the year, presents me with
A brace of horses: two such steeds might well
Be by a pair of kings back'd, in a field[333]
That their crowns' titles tried. Alas, alas,
Poor cousin Palamon, poor prisoner, thou
So little dream'st upon my fortune that
Thou think'st thyself the happier thing, to be
So near Emilia: me thou deem'st at Thebes,
And therein wretched, although free; but if
Thou knew'st my mistress breath'd on me, and that
I ear'd[334] her language, liv'd in her eye, O coz,
What passion[335] would enclose thee.

#2 Male—Dramatic
   Wooer: an observant commoner, 20s

   When the Wooer discovers the daughter of the royal jailer wandering in the woods,
   he wastes no time in reporting this to her father.

WOOER: I'll tell you quickly. As I late was angling
In the great lake that lies behind the palace,
From the far shore, thick set with reeds and sedges,
As patiently I was attending sport,[336]
I heard a voice, a shrill one, and attentive
I gave my ear, when I might well perceive
'Twas one that sung, and by the smallness[337] of it
A boy or woman. I then left my angle[338]
To his own skill, came near, but yet perceiv'd not
Who made the sound, the rushes and the reeds
Had so encompass'd it. I laid me down
And listen'd to the words she sung, for then,
Through a small glade[339] cut by the fishermen,
I saw it was your daughter.

....

332best
333battlefield
334heard
335anger
336concentrating on my fishing
337softness
338fishing tackle
339passage

[*JAILER:* Pray go on, sir.]
WOOER: She sung much, but no sense; only I heard her
Repeat this often: "Palamon is gone,
Is gone to th' wood to gather mulberries;
I'll find him out tomorrow."
[*FIRST FRIEND:* Pretty soul!]
WOOER: "His shackles will betray him, he'll be taken,
And what shall I do then? I'll bring a bevy,[340]
A hundred black-eyed maids that love as I do,
With chaplets[341] on their heads of daffadillies,
With cherry lips and cheeks of damask[342] roses,
And all we'll dance an antic[343] 'fore the duke
And beg his pardon." Then she talk'd of you, sir;
That you must lose your head tomorrow morning,
And she must gather flowers to bury you,
And see the house made handsome. Then she sung
Nothing but "Willow, willow, willow,"[344] and between
Ever was "Palamon, fair Palamon,"
And "Palamon was a tall[345] young man." The place
Was knee-deep[346] where she sat; her careless tresses
A wreath of bullrush rounded; about her stuck
Thousand fresh water flowers of several colors;
That methought she appear'd like the fair nymph
That feeds the lake with waters, or as Iris[347]
Newly dropp'd down from heaven. Rings she made
Of rushes[348] that grew by, and to 'em spoke
The prettiest posies:[349] "Thus our true love's tied,"
"This you may lose, not me," and many a one;
And then she wept, and sung again, and sigh'd,

---

[340]company
[341]garlands
[342]Deep pink or light red.
[343]Alluding to her participation in the morris in III.v.
[344]Refrain of a song best known from the adaptation in *Othello*, IV.iii; Chappell, 207.
[345]Brave, handsome.
[346]With rushes.
[347]Messenger of Juno; goddess of the rainbow.
[348]Rush-rings were used by country people as keepsakes or wedding rings.
[349]Mottoes inscribed on rings.

And with the same breath smil'd and kiss'd her hand.
[SECOND FRIEND: Alas, what pity it is!]
WOOER: I made in to her:
She saw me and straight sought the flood; I sav'd her
And set her safe to land; when presently
She slipp'd away and to the city made,
With such a cry and swiftness that, believe me,
She left me far behind her. Three or four
I saw from far off cross[350] her; one of 'em
I knew to be your brother; where she stayed and fell,
Scarce to be got away. I left them with her,
And hither came to tell you.

#3 Male—Dramatic
Arcite

> As Arcite prepares to meet Palamon in a deadly tournament that will decide which
> of the two knights will gain Emilia's hand in marriage, he pauses to pray to Mars,
> the god of war.

ARCITE: Knights, kinsmen, lovers, yea, my sacrifices,
True worshippers of Mars, whose spirit in you
Expels the seeds of fear and th'apprehension[351]
Which still is further[352] of it, go with me
Before the god of our profession. There
Require[353] of him the hearts of lions and
The breath of tigers, yea, the fierceness too,
Yea, the speed also—to go on, I mean,
Else wish we to be snails. You know my prize
Must be dragg'd out of blood; force and great feat[354]
Must put my garland[355] on me, where she sticks,
The queen of flowers. Our intercession, then,
Must be to him that makes the camp[356] a cistern

---

[350]meet
[351]anticipation
[352]Rare form of "furtherer," encourager.
[353]request
[354]deed
[355]Prize; referring both to the victor's crown and to Emilia.
[356]battlefield

Brimm'd with the blood of men: give me your aid,
And bend your spirits towards him. (*They kneel.*)
Thou mighty one, that with thy power hast turn'd
Green Neptune into purple; whose approach
Comets prewarn; whose havoc in vast field
Unearthed skulls proclaim; whose breath blows down
The teeming[357] Ceres' foison;[358] who dost pluck,
With hand armipotent,[359] from forth blue clouds[360]
The mason'd turrets, that both mak'st and break'st
The stony girths[361] of cities; me thy pupil,
Youngest follower of thy drum, instruct this day
With military skill, that to thy laud[362]
I may advance my streamer[363] and by thee
Be styl'd[364] the lord o'th' day. Give me, great Mars,
Some token of thy pleasure.
(*Here they fall on their faces, as formerly,[365] and there is heard clanging of armor, with a short thunder, as the burst of a battle, whereupon they all rise and bow to the altar.*)
O great corrector of enormous[366] times,
Shaker of o'er rank states, thou grand decider
Of dusty and old titles, that heal'st with blood
The earth when it is sick,[367] and cur'st the world
O'th' pleurisy[368] of people, I do take
Thy signs auspiciously and in thy name
To my design march boldly.— Let us go.

---

[357]productive
[358]Plentiful harvest.
[359]Mighty in arms.
[360]Clouds of smoke.
[361]walls
[362]praise
[363]banner
[364]named
[365]Apparently referring to an earlier piece of action, perhaps at l. 48, for which no stage directions survives.
[366]disordered
[367]For the idea of war as a healer.
[368]Excess; an incorrect etymology derived the word from Latin *plus*, more, rather than from Greek *pleura*, side.

Palamon: a knight of Thebes, 20s

On the eve of a tournament that will determine who shall wed the lovely Emilia, Palamon offers a prayer to the gods.

PALAMON: Our stars must glister with new fire, or be
Today extinct; our argument is love,
Which if the goddess of it grant, she gives
Victory too: then blend your spirits with mine,
You, whose free nobleness do make my cause
Your personal hazard. To the goddess Venus
Commend we our proceeding, and implore
Her power unto our party.
(*Here they kneel as formerly.*)
Hail, sovereign queen of secrets, who hast power
To call the fiercest tyrant from his rage
And weep[369] unto a girl; that hast the might,
Even with an eye-glance, to choke Mars's drum
And turn th'alarm[370] to whispers; that canst make
A cripple flourish with his crutch, and cure him
Before Apollo,[371] that mayst force the king
To be his subject's vassal, and induce
Stale gravity to dance; the poll'd[372] bachelor—
Whose youth like wanton boys through bonfires,[373]
Have skipp'd[374] thy flame—at seventy thou canst catch,
And make him, to the scorn of his hoarse throat,
Abuse young lays of love. What godlike power
Hast thou not power upon? To Phoebus thou
Add'st flames hotter than his: the heavenly fires
Did scorch his mortal son,[375] thine him; the huntress,
All moist and cold, some say, began to throw

---

[369]And to make him weep for love.
[370]Call to arms.
[371]God of healing.
[372]bald
[373]J. G. Frazer, *The Golden Bough* (abridged ed., London, 1957), ch. lxii, records the widespread practice of jumping over the fire at spring and midsummer festivals.
[374](1) jumped over; (2) escaped.
[375]Phaëton.

Her bow away and sigh.[376] Take to thy grace
Me, thy vow'd soldier, who do bear thy yoke
As 'twere a wreath of roses, yet is heavier
Than lead itself, stings more than nettles.
I have never been foul-mouth'd against thy law;
Ne'er reveal'd secret, for I knew none; would not,
Had I kenn'd[377] all that were; I never practiced
Upon[378] man's wife, nor would the libels read
Of liberal[379] wits; I never at great feasts
Sought to betray a beauty, but have blush'd
At simp'ring sirs that did; I have been harsh
To large confessors,[380] and have hotly[381] ask'd them
If they had mothers—I had one, a woman,
And women 'twere they wrong'd. I knew a man
Of eighty winters, this I told them, who
A lass of fourteen brided. "Twas thy power
To put life into dust: the aged cramp
Had screw'd his square[382] foot round,[383]
The gout had knit his fingers into knots,
Torturing convulsions from his globy eyes
Had almost drawn their spheres,[384] that what was life
In him seem'd torture; this anatomy[385]
Had by his young fair fere[386] a boy, and I
Believ'd it was his, for she swore it was,
And who would not believe her? Brief, I am
To those that prate and have done,[387] no companion;
To those that boast and have not, a defier;
To those that would and cannot, a rejoicer.

---

[376]Alluding to the love of Diana for Endymion; see M. Drayton, *Endymion and Phoebe*.
[377]known
[378]deceived
[379]licentious
[380]Boasters in public.
[381]angrily
[382]sturdy
[383]Bent with age.
[384]Had almost pulled the sockets from his eyes.
[385]skeleton
[386]wife
[387]Kiss and tell.

Yea, him I do not love, that tells close offices[388]
The foulest way, nor names concealments[389] in
The boldest language: such a one I am,
And vow that lover never yet made sign
Truer than I. O then, most soft sweet goddess,
Give me the victory of this question, which
Is true love's merit,[390] and bless me with a sign
Of thy great pleasure.
(*Here music is heard [and] doves are seen to flutter. They fall again upon their*
faces, then on their knees.)
O thou that from eleven to ninety reign'st
In mortal bosoms, whose chase is this world[391]
And we in herds thy game, I give thee thanks
For this fair token, which, being laid unto
Mine innocent true heart, arms in assurance
My body to this business.— Let us rise
And bow before the goddess. (*They bow.*) Time comes on.

---

[388]Secret functions.
[389]Things that should be concealed.
[390]Due reward.
[391]Hunting ground.

The Winter's Tale

William Shakespeare
1611

Scene: Sicilia

Male—Dramatic
    Antigonus: a lord of Sicilia, 30s

> The Queen of Sicilia has been charged with high treason and adultery for bearing a
> child the king refuses to believe is his own. Although the Delphic Oracle has
> proclaimed the queen's innocence, the king has demanded that the infant be aban-
> doned on the desolate shore of Bohemia. Lord Antigonus has been charged with this
> unhappy task, and here wishes the baby well as he sets her ashore.

ANTIGONUS: Come, poor babe:
I have heard, but not believed, the spirits o' the dead
May walk again: if such thing be, thy mother
Appear'd to me last night, for ne'er was dream
So like a waking. To me comes a creature,
Sometimes her head on one side, some another;
I never saw a vessel of like sorrow,
So fill'd and so becoming: in pure white robes,
Like very sanctity, she did approach
My cabin where I lay; thrice bow'd before me,
And gasping to begin some speech, her eyes
Became two spouts: the fury spent, anon
Did this break from her: "Good Antigonous,
Since fate, against thy better disposition,
Hath made thy person for the thrower-out
Of my poor babe, according to thine oath,
Places remote enough are in Bohemia,
There weep and leave it crying; and, for the babe
Is counted lost for ever, Perdita,
I prithee, call't. For this ungentle business,
Put on thee by my lord, thou ne'er shalt see
Thy wife Paulina more." And so, with shrieks,
She melted into air. Affrighted much,
I did in time collect myself and thought
This was so and no slumber. Dreams are toys:

Yet for this once, yea, superstitiously,
I will be squared by this. I do believe
Hermione hath suffer'd death, and that
Apollo would, this being indeed the issue
Of King Polixenes, it should here be laid,
Either for life or death, upon the earth
Of its right father. Blossom, speed thee well!
There lie, and there thy character: there these;
Which may, if fortune please, both breed thee, pretty,
And still rest thine. The storm begins: poor wretch,
That for thy mother's fault art thus exposed
To loss and what may follow! Weep I cannot,
But my heart bleeds; and most accursed am I
To be by oath enjoin'd to this. Farewell!
The day frowns more and more: thou'rt like to have
A lullaby too rough: I never saw
The heavens so dim by day. A savage clamour!
Well may I get aboard! This is the case:
I am gone for ever.

The Witch

Thomas Middleton
1619–27

Scene: Ravenna

Male—Serio-Comic
    Almachildes: a ladies' man, 30–40

> Following an evening of drunken revelry, Almachildes foolishly purchased a love charm from a witch. In the sober light of day, he takes a moment to examine his strange new possession.

ALMACHILDES: What a mad toy took me to sup with witches?
Fie of all drunken humours! By this hand
I could beat myself when I think on't; and the rascals
Made me good cheer too; and to my understanding then
Ate some of every dish, and spoiled the rest.
But coming to my lodging, I remember
I was as hungry as a tired foot-post.
What's this? (*Takes from his pocket a ribbon.*)
    O, 'tis the charm her hagship gave me
For my duchess' obstinate woman; wound about
A threepenny silk ribbon of three colours,
Necte tribus nodis ternos Amoretta colores.
Amoretta!—why, there's her name indeed.
Necte—*Amoretta*—again, two boughts;
Nodo et Veneris dic vincula necte.
Nay, if Veneris be one, I'm sure there's no dead flesh in't.
If I should undertake to construe this now,
I should make a fine piece of work of it,
For few young gallants are given to good construction
Of anything, hardly of their best friends' wives,
Sisters or nieces. Let me see what I can do now.
Necte tribus nodis—Nick of the tribe of noddies;
Ternos colores—that makes turned colours;
Nodo et Veneris—goes to his venery like a noddy;
Dic vincula—with Dick the vintner's boy.
Here were a sweet charm now, if this were the meaning on't; and very

likely to overcome an honourable gentlewoman. The whoreson old hellcat would have given me the brain of a cat once, in my handkerchief—I bad her make sauce with't with a vengeance!—and a little bone in the nethermost part of a wolf's tail—I bad her pick her teeth with't, with a pestilence! Nay this is somewhat cleanly yet and handsome—a coloured ribbon? A fine, gentle charm; a man may give't his sister, his brother's wife, ordinarily. See, here she comes luckily.

Women Beware Women

Thomas Middleton
1657

Scene: Florence

Male—Serio-Comic
> Leantio: a young man in love with his wife, 20s

> As he returns home after a day's work, Leantio extols the virtues and joys of matrimony.

LEANTIO: How near am I now to a happiness,
That earth exceeds not! not another like it;
The treasures of the deep are not so precious,
As are the conceal'd comforts of a man,
Lockt up in woman's love. I scent the air
Of blessings when I come but near the house;
What a delicious breath marriage sends forth!
The violet-bed's not sweeter. Honest wedlock
Is like a banqueting-house built in a garden,
On which the spring's chaste flowers take delight
To cast their modest odours; when base lust,
With all her powders, paintings, and best pride,
Is but a fair house built by a ditch-side.
When I behold a glorious dangerous strumpet,
Sparkling in beauty and destruction too,
Both at a twinkling, I do liken straight
Her beautifi'd body to a goodly temple
That's built on vaults where carcasses lie rotting,
And so by little and little I shrink back again,
And quench desire with a cool meditation,
And I'm as well methinks. Now for a welcome
Able to draw men's envies upon man:
A kiss now that will hang upon my lip,
As sweet as morning dew upon a rose,
And full as long; after a five days' fast
She'll be so greedy now, and cling about me,
I take care how I shall be rid of her;
And here't begins.

The Wonder of Women or
The Tragedy of Sophonisba

John Marston
1606

Scene: Libya

Male—Dramatic
  Syphax: King of Libya, 30s

> When Syphax is rejected by Sophonisba, a princess of Carthage, he flies into a rage
> and joins with the great Roman general, Scipio, who plans to invade Carthage.

SYPHAX: To Carthage, Carthage! O thou eternal youth,
Man of large fame, great and abounding glory,
Renownful Scipio, spread thy two-necked eagles,
Fill full thy sails with a revenging wind,
Strike through obedient Neptune till thy prows
Dash up our Libyan ooze and thy just arms
Shine with amazeful terror on these walls!
O now record thy father's honoured blood
Which Carthage drunk; thy uncle Pubius' blood
Which Carthage drunk; three hundred hundred souls
Of choice Italians Carthage set on wing.
Remember Hannibal, yet Hannibal,
The consul-queller. O then enlarge thy heart,
Be thousand souls in one! Let all the breath,
The spirit of thy name and nation, be mixed strong
In thy great heart! O fall like thunder-shaft,
The winged vengeance of incensèd Jove
Upon this Carthage! For Syphax here flies off
From all allegiance, from all love or service,
His now freed sceptre once did yield this city.
Ye universal gods, light, heat, and air
Prove all unblessing Syphax if his hands
Once rear themselves for Carthage but to curse it!
It had been better they had changed their faith,
Denied their gods, than slighted Syphax' love,

So fearfully will I take vengeance.
I'll interleague with Scipio.— Vangue,
Dear Ethiopian negro, go wing a vessel,
And fly to Scipio. Say his confederate,
Vowed and confirmed, is Syphax. Bid him haste
To mix our palms and arms. Will him make up,
Whilst we are in the strength of discontent,
Our unsuspected forces well in arms.
For Sophonisba, Carthage, Asdrubal,
Shall feel their weakness in preferring weakness
And one less great than we. To our dear wishes
Haste, gentle negro, that this heap may know
Me and their wrong.

[*VANGUE:* Wrong?]

SYPHAX: Ay, though 'twere not, yet know while kings are strong,
What they'll but think, and not what is, is wrong.
I am disgraced in and by that which hath
No reason—love, and woman. My revenge
Shall therefore bear no argument of right:
Passion is reason when it speaks from might.
I tell thee, man, nor kings nor gods exempt,
But they grow pale if once they find contempt.
Haste!